The Ballerina of Auschwitz

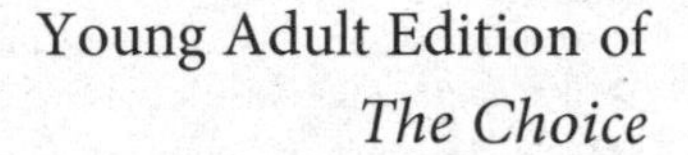

Young Adult Edition of
The Choice

THE Ballerina OF Auschwitz

Dr. Edith Eva Eger
with Esmé Schwall
edited by Jordan Engle

atheneum
New York London Toronto Sydney New Delhi

An imprint of Simon & Schuster Children's Publishing Division
1230 Avenue of the Americas, New York, New York 10020
This work is a memoir. It reflects the author's present recollections of her experiences over a period of years.

Jacket design by Debra Sfetsios-Conover
This young readers edition is adapted from *The Choice* by Dr. Edith Eva Eger, published by Scribner in 2017

Simon & Schuster: Celebrating 100 Years of Publishing in 2024
For information about special discounts for bulk purchases, please contact Simon & Schuster Special Sales at 1-866-506-1949 or business@simonandschuster.com.
The Simon & Schuster Speakers Bureau can bring authors to your live event. For more information or to book an event, contact the Simon & Schuster Speakers Bureau at 1-866-248-3049 or visit our website at www.simonspeakers.com.
Interior design by Irene Metaxatos
The text for this book was set in Minion Pro.
Manufactured in the United States of America
First Edition
10 9 8 7 6 5 4 3 2 1
Library of Congress Cataloging-in-Publication Data
Names: Eger, Edith Eva, author. | Schwall, Esmé, author. | Eger, Edith Eva. Choice.
Title: The ballerina of Auschwitz / Dr. Edith Eva Eger, with Esmé Schwall.
Description: First edition. | New York, NY : Atheneum Books for Young Readers, [2024] | Young adult edition of "The Choice." | Audience: Ages 12 up | Summary: "Edie is a talented dancer and skilled gymnast with hopes of making the Olympics. Between her rigorous training and her struggle to find her place in a family where she's considered the daughter 'with brains but no looks,' Edie's too busy to dwell on the state of the world. But life in Hungary in 1943 is dangerous for a Jewish girl. Just as Edie falls in love for the first time, Europe collapses into war, and Edie's family is forced onto a train bound for the Auschwitz concentration camp. Even in that darkest of moments, Edie's beloved, Eric, kindles hope. 'I'll never forget your eyes,' he tells her through the slats of the cattle car. Auschwitz is horrifying beyond belief, yet through starvation and unthinkable terrors, dreams of Eric sustain Edie. Against all odds, Edie and her sister Magda survive, thanks to their sisterhood and sheer grit. In this young adult edition of her bestselling, award-winning memoir 'The Choice,' renowned psychologist and Holocaust survivor Dr. Edith Eger gives readers a gift of hope and strength"—Provided by publisher.
Identifiers: LCCN 2024004686 | ISBN 9781665952552 (hardcover) | ISBN 9781665952576 (ebook)
Subjects: LCSH: Eger, Edith Eva—Juvenile literature. | Auschwitz (Concentration camp)—Juvenile literature. | Psychologists—United States—Biography—Juvenile literature. | Holocaust, Jewish (1939–1945)—Personal narratives—Juvenile literature. | Holocaust survivors—United States—Biography—Juvenile literature.
Classification: LCC BF109.E37 A3 2024 | DDC 940.53/18092 [B]—dc23/eng/20240531
LC record available at https://lccn.loc.gov/2024004686

For the five generations of my family:

my father, Lajos, who taught me to laugh;
my mother, Ilona, who helped me find what I needed inside;
my gorgeous and unbelievable sisters, Magda and Klara;
my children: Marianne, Audrey, and John;
and their children: Lindsey, Jordan, Rachel, David, and Ashley;
and their children's children: Silas, Graham, Hale, Noah,
Dylan, Marcos, and Rafael.

And to my readers, young and old:

there will never be another you. May love steer your life.

AUTHOR'S NOTE

Dear Reader, I've been writing this book for nearly eighty years. When I was sixteen, enduring firsthand the horrors of the Holocaust; as I witnessed my children—and then my grandchildren and great-grandchildren—come of age; as I taught high school students and became a psychologist specializing in treating trauma; as I connected with my many beloved patients and audiences around the world, I was aready writing to you in my mind. I was longing to share with you the tools that helped me survive the unthinkable, longing for you to know that a story of humans' capacity for evil is also a story of our inexorable capacity for hope.

I feel a responsibility to share my story. To tell the truth about what happened so that we don't ever forget—and also to share a legacy of hope and zest for life so that my parents and millions of others didn't die in vain. I want the triumph and celebration of life to live on.

This feels like the right moment to finally share my story with you. A little over a year ago, my sister Magda died—just a few weeks after her hundredth birthday. I realized that if I didn't write this book for you now, I might miss my chance. So I'm motivated by my own mortality.

I'm also motivated by *your* life. I see the big challenges you face in today's world, troubling realities such as gun violence, cyberbullying, climate change, a global pandemic, shockingly high rates of anxiety, depression, despair, suicide. I want to use my ninety-six years on this planet, my near century of life and evolution and healing, to be your cheerleader and advocate. To offer you an emotional and spiritual blueprint for coming to terms with the inevitable pain and struggle you will encounter. And I want to give you something written especially for you at this stage of your becoming, as you accept what you've inherited and endured, and embrace your strength and authenticity, and choose to build the life you most want to live.

I gratefully offer this book to you now in the hope that you will read my story and feel that you are not alone in this strange work of being human. In the hope that you will read my story and think, *If she can do it, so can I!* I offer you this book so that you too can transcend victimhood and choose to dance through life, even in hellish circumstances. I give you my story to empower you to be an ambassador of peace and an agent of choice in your life. I give you this book so that you can live as you truly are: precious and free.

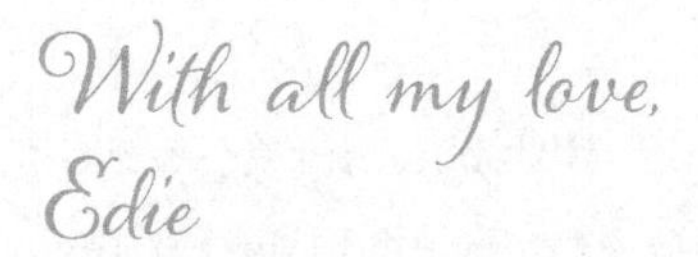

October 2024

PROLOGUE

If I could distill my entire life into one moment, into one still image, it is this: three women in dark wool coats wait, arms linked, in a barren yard. They are exhausted. They've got dust on their shoes. They stand in a long line.

The three women are my mother, my sister Magda, and me. This is our last moment together. We don't know that. We refuse to consider it. Or we are too weary even to speculate about what is ahead. It is a moment of severing—mother from daughters, life as it has been from all that will come after. And yet only hindsight can give it this meaning.

I see the three of us from behind, as though I am next in line. Why does memory give me the back of my mother's head but not her face? Her long hair is intricately braided and clipped on top of her head. Magda's light brown waves touch her shoulders. My dark hair is tucked under a scarf. My mother stands in the middle, and Magda and I both lean inward. It is impossible to discern if we are the ones who keep our mother upright, or if it is the other way around, her strength the pillar that supports Magda and me.

This moment is a threshold into the major losses of my life. For eight decades I have returned again and again to this image of the three of us. I have studied it as though with enough scrutiny I can recover something precious. As though I can regain the life that precedes this moment, the life that precedes loss. As if there is such a thing. As if I can return to this time when our arms are joined and we belong to one another. I see our sloped shoulders. The dust holding to the bottoms of our coats. My mother. My sister. Me.

Chapter 1
THE LITTLE ONE

They wanted a boy, but they got me.

A girl. A third daughter, the runt of the family.

"I'm glad you have brains because you have no looks," my mother often tells me. Maybe she means that I'll never be beautiful. Or maybe this compliment wrapped in criticism is her way of encouraging me to study hard. Motivation expressed as caution. Maybe there's some invisible fate she's trying to spare me. Maybe she's trying to give me some better idea of who I might become. "You can learn to cook some other time," she told me when I asked her to teach me to braid challah or fry chicken or make the cherry jam she preserves in summer and tucks away for the rest of the year. "You go back to school."

Today, I stand in front of the mirror in the bathroom in our apartment, brushing my teeth, getting ready for school. I study my reflection. Is it true that I have no looks? I'm a dancer and a gymnast, my body lean and muscular. I like my strength. I like my wavy brown hair—though Magda, my oldest sister, is the pretty one. But when I meet my own eyes in the mirror, when I sink into that mysterious and familiar blue green, I can't put my finger on what I see. It's like I'm on the outside of my life, looking in, watching myself like a character in a novel, her destiny unknown, her heart and self still unfolding.

I've just finished reading one of my mother's novels, Émile Zola's *Nana*, pilfered from her bookshelf and devoured in secret. I can't get the last scene out of my head. Nana, the beautiful, chic performer, the one who was desired by so many men, lies broken and diseased, her body erupted in smallpox sores. There's something terrifying in the way her body is described. Even before the smallpox, even when she was still gorgeous and charming, her body was dangerous. A weapon. Threatening, something of which to beware.

Yet she was wanted. I'm hungry for a love like that. To be seen and known as a treasure. To be showered with affection, savored like a feast.

Instead, I'm taught caution.

"Washing up is like doing the dishes," my mother has told me. "Start with the crystal, then work your way down to the pots and pans." Save the dirtiest for last. Even my own body is suspect.

Magda raps on the bathroom door, tired of waiting her turn.

"Stop dreaming, Dicuka," she complains. She uses the pet name my mother invented for me. Ditzu-ka. These nonsense syllables are usually warmth to me. Today they are harsh and clanging.

I hurry past my irritated sister toward our shared bedroom to dress, still thinking of the girl in the mirror—the girl longing for love. Maybe the kind of love I crave is impossible. I have spent thirteen years stitching together my memories and experiences into a story of who I am, a story that seems to reveal that I'm damaged, that I'm not wanted, that I don't belong.

Like the night when I was seven and my parents hosted a dinner party. They sent me out of the room to refill a pitcher of water, and from the kitchen I heard them joke, "We could have saved that one." They meant that before I came along, they were already a complete family. They had Magda, who played piano, and Klara, the violin prodigy. I didn't bring anything new to the table. I was unnecessary, not good enough. There was no room for me.

I tested this theory when I was eight and decided to run away. I would see if my parents even knew I was gone. Instead of going to school, I took the trolley to my grandparents' house. I trusted my grandparents—my mother's father and stepmother—to cover for me. They engaged in a continuous war with my mother on Magda's behalf, hiding cookies in my sister's dresser drawer. They were safety to me. They held hands, something my own parents never did. They were pure comfort—the smell of brisket and baked beans, of sweet bread, of cholent, a rich stew that my grandmother brought to the bakery to cook on Sabbath, when Orthodox practice did not permit her to use her own oven.

My grandparents were happy to see me. I didn't have to perform for their love or approval. It was freely given, and we spent a wonderful morning in the kitchen, eating nut rolls. But then the doorbell rang. My grandfather went to answer it. A moment later he rushed into the kitchen. He was hard of hearing, and he spoke his warning too loudly. "Hide, Dicuka!" he yelled. "Your mother's here!" In trying to protect me, he gave me away.

What bothered me the most was the look on my mother's face when she saw me in my grandparents' kitchen. It's not just that she was surprised to see me here—it was as though the very fact of my existence had taken her by surprise. As though I was not who she wanted or expected me to be.

Yet I am often her companion, sitting in the kitchen with her when my dad is away on business trips to Paris, filling suitcases with silk for his tailoring business, my mother rigid and watchful when he returns, worried that he's spent too much money. She doesn't invite friends over for visits. There's no easy gossip in the parlor, no discussions of books or politics. I'm the one to whom my mother tells her secrets. I cherish the time I spend alone with her.

One evening when I was nine, we were alone in the kitchen. She was wrapping up the leftover strudel that she'd made with dough I'd watched her cut by hand and drape like heavy linen over the dining room table. "Read to me," she said, and I fetched the worn copy of *Gone with the Wind* from her bedside table. We had read it through once before. We'd begun again. I paused over the mysterious inscription, written in English, on the title page of the translated book. It was in a man's handwriting, but not my father's. All that my mother would say is that the book was a gift from a man she met when she worked at the Foreign Ministry before she knew my father.

We sat in straight-backed chairs near the woodstove. When we read together, I didn't have to share her with anyone else. I sank into the words and the story and the feeling of being alone in a world with her. Scarlett returns to Tara at the end of the war to learn her mother is dead and her father is far gone in grief. "*As God is my witness,*" Scarlett says, "*I'm never going to be hungry again.*" My mother closed her eyes and leaned her head against the back of the chair. I wanted to climb into her lap. I wanted to rest my head against her chest. I wanted her to touch her lips to my hair.

"Tara . . . ," she said. "America, now that would be a place to see." I wished she would say my name with the same softness she reserves for a country where she's never been. All the delicious smells of my mother's kitchen were mixed up for me with the drama of hunger and feast—always, even in the feast, that longing. I didn't know if the longing was hers or mine or something we shared.

We sat with the fire between us.

"When I was your age . . . ," she began.

Now that she was talking, I was afraid to move, afraid she wouldn't continue if I did.

"When I was your age, the babies slept together, and my mother and I shared a bed. One morning I woke up because my father was calling to me, 'Ilonka, wake up your mother. She hasn't made breakfast yet or laid out my clothes.' I turned to my mother next to me under the covers. But she wasn't moving. She was dead."

I wanted to know every detail about this moment when a

daughter woke beside a mother she had already lost. I also wanted to look away. It was too terrifying to think about.

"When they buried her that afternoon, I thought they had put her in the ground alive. That night, Father told me to make the family supper. So that's what I did."

I waited for the rest of the story. I waited for the lesson at the end, or the reassurance.

"Bedtime" was all my mother said. She bent to sweep the ash under the stove.

Footsteps thumped down the hall outside our door. I could smell my father's tobacco even before I heard the jangle of his keys.

"Ladies," he called, "are you still awake?" He came into the kitchen in his shiny shoes and dapper suit, his big grin, a little sack in his hand that he gave me with a loud kiss to the forehead. "I won again," he boasted. Whenever he played cards or billiards with his friends, he shared the spoils with me. That night he'd brought a petit four laced in pink icing. If I were my sister Magda, my mother, always concerned about Magda's weight, would snatch the treat away, but she nodded at me, giving me permission to eat it.

She stood up, on her way from the fire to the sink. My father intercepted her, lifted her hand so he could twirl her around the room, which she did, stiffly, without a smile. He pulled her in for an embrace, one hand on her back, one teasing at her breast. My mother shrugged him away.

"I'm a disappointment to your mother," my father half whispered to me as we left the kitchen. Did he intend for her to overhear, or was this a secret meant only for me? Either way, it is something I stored away to mull over later. Yet the bitterness in his voice scared me. "She wants to go to the opera every night, live some fancy cosmopolitan life. I'm just a tailor. A tailor and a billiards player."

My father's defeated tone confused me. He is well known in our town, and well liked. Playful, smiling, he always seems comfortable and alive and fun to be around. He goes out with his many friends. He loves food—especially the ham he sometimes smuggles into our household, eating it over the newspaper it is wrapped in, pushing bites of forbidden pork into my mouth, enduring my mother's accusations that he is a poor role model. His tailor shop has won two gold medals. He isn't just a maker of even seams and straight hems. He is a master of couture. That's how he met my mother—she came into his shop because she needed a dress, and his work came so highly recommended. But he had wanted to be a doctor, not a tailor, a dream his father had discouraged, and every once in a while, his disappointment in himself surfaced.

"You're not just a tailor, Papa," I reassured him. "You're a famous dress designer!"

"And you're going to be the best-dressed lady in Košice," he told me, patting my head. "You have the perfect figure for couture."

He'd pushed his disappointment back into the shadows. We stood together in the hall, neither one of us quite ready to break away.

"I wanted you to be a boy, you know," my father said. "I slammed the door when you were born. I was that mad at having another girl. But now you're the only one I can talk to." He kissed my forehead.

I still love my father's attention. Like my mother's, it is precious . . . and precarious. As though my worthiness of their love has less to do with me and more to do with their loneliness. As though my identity isn't about anything that I am or have and only a measure of what each of my parents is missing.

When I join my family at the breakfast table, my older sisters greet me with the song they invented for me when I was three and one of my eyes became crossed in a botched medical procedure. "You're so ugly, you're so puny," they sing. "You'll never find a husband."

For years, I turned my head toward the ground when I walked so that I didn't have to see anyone looking at my lopsided face. I had surgery when I was ten to correct the crossed eye, and now I should be able to lift my head and smile when I meet strangers, yet the self-consciousness persists, helped along by my sisters' teasing.

Magda is nineteen, with sensual lips and wavy hair. She is the jokester in our family. When we were younger, she showed me how to drop grapes out of our bedroom window into the coffee cups of the patrons sitting on the patio below. Klara, the middle sister, the violin prodigy, mastered the Mendelssohn violin concerto when she was five.

I am used to being the silent sister, the invisible one. I'm so convinced of my inferiority that I rarely introduce myself by name. "I am Klara's sister," I say. It doesn't occur to me that Magda might tire of being the clown, that Klara might resent being the prodigy. She can't stop being extraordinary, not for a second, or everything might be taken from her—the adoration she's accustomed to, her very sense of self. Magda and I have to work at getting something we are certain there will never be enough of; Klara has to worry that at any moment she might make a fatal mistake and lose it all. Klara has been playing violin all my life, since she was three. Often she stands in front of an open window to practice, as though she can't fully enjoy her creative genius unless she can summon an audience of passersby to witness it. It seems that for her, love is not boundless, it's conditional—the reward for a performance, what you settle for. And there's a price to being loved: the work of being accepted and adored is in the end a kind of vanishing.

We eat buns from the bakery down the street smothered in butter and my mother's apricot jam, more sweet than sour. My mother pours coffee and hands food around the table. My father has already hung a tape measure around his neck and tucked a piece of chalk in his breast pocket for marking fabric. Magda waits for my mother to offer a second helping of buns. "Take it. I'll eat it," she always urges me if I decline a second helping. Klara clears her throat, and everyone turns in her direction to hear what she will say.

"I have to reply to the professor about the invitation to study in New York," she says, her knife smoothing the soft butter across the warm bread.

"We have family in New York," my father muses, stirring his coffee. He means his sister Matilda, who lives in a place called the Bronx, in a Jewish immigrant neighborhood.

"No," my mother says. "We've already discussed this. America is too far away."

I think of that long-ago night in the kitchen when she spoke of America with such yearning. Maybe this is what life is, a constant waffling between the things we don't have but wish we did and the things we have but wish we didn't.

Klara squares her jaw. "If not New York," she says, "then Budapest."

My mother drops her head as she clears plates from the table. To support the career of the favorite child means losing her. Or maybe it's not the idea of Klarie leaving home that makes her sad; maybe it's her own intransigence. Maybe she's angry with herself for saying no when she wants to be saying yes.

My father's chronic good mood is unperturbed by the weight of Klara's decision or the worry with which my mother carries it.

"We'll talk about it," he says, dispatching the somber mood that's descended once again over our family table. Then he turns to me. "Dicuka," he says, handing me an envelope, "bring this money to school. Tuition's due."

I hold the envelope in my hand, feeling the significance of his trust. Yet his handing over of this responsibility is also an admonishment. A reminder of what I cost the family. An open question about the value I bring. I hold tightly to the envelope as I gather my things for school, as though my grip on it will help me to pinpoint how much I matter and how much I don't, as though it will help me to draw the map that shows the dimensions and the borders of my worth.

I am happiest when I am alone, when I can retreat into my inner world, and the walk to the private Jewish school I attend is time I prize. I practice the steps to "The Blue Danube" routine my ballet class will perform at a festival on the river.

I think of my ballet master and his wife, of the feeling I get when I take the steps up to the studio two or three at a time and kick off my school clothes, pull on my leotard and tights. I have been studying ballet since I was five years old, since my mother intuited that I wasn't a musician, that I had other gifts. (My parents had tried to start me on Klara's old violin, but it didn't take long before my mother was pulling the instrument out of my hands, saying, "That's enough.") Ballet, though—I loved it from the start. My aunt and uncle gave me a tutu that I wore to my first lesson. Somehow, I didn't feel shy in the studio. I walked straight up to the pianist who played music for the class to dance to and asked what pieces he planned to play. "Go dance, honey," he told me. "I'll take care of the piano."

By the time I was eight, I was going to ballet classes three times a week. I liked doing something that was all mine, different from my sisters. And I liked being in my body. I liked practicing the splits, our ballet master reminding us that strength and flexibility are inseparable—for one muscle to flex, another must open; to achieve length and limberness, we have to hold our cores strong. I held his instructions in my mind like a prayer. Down I went, spine straight, abdominal muscles tight, legs stretching apart. I knew to breathe, especially when I felt stuck. I pictured my body expanding like the strings on my sister's violin, finding the exact place of tautness that made the whole instrument ring. And then I was down. I was there. In the full splits. "Brava!" My ballet master clapped. "Stay right as you are." He lifted me off the ground and over his head. It was hard to keep my legs fully extended without the floor to push against, but for a moment I felt like an offering. I felt like pure light. "Editke," my teacher said, "all your ecstasy in life is going to come from the inside." I don't yet really understand what he meant. But I know that I can breathe and spin and kick and bend. That as my muscles stretch and strengthen, every movement, every pose seems to call out: *I am, I am, I am. I am me. I am somebody.*

Invention takes hold, and I am off and away in a new dance of my own, one in which I imagine my parents meeting. I dance both of their parts. My father does a slapstick double-take when he sees my mother walk into the room. My mother spins faster, leaps higher. I make my whole body arc into a joyful laugh. I have never seen my mother rejoice, never heard her laugh from the belly, but in my body, I feel the untapped well of her happiness.

When I get to school, the tuition money my father gave me to cover an entire quarter of school is gone. Somehow, in the flurry of dancing, I have lost it. I check every pocket and crease of my clothing, but it is gone. All day the dread of telling my father burns like ice in my gut.

At home that night, I wait till after dinner to muster the courage to tell my father what I've done. He can't look at me as he raises his fist, gripping a belt. This is the first time he has ever hit me, or any of us. He doesn't say a word to me when he is done.

I crawl into bed early, before my homework is finished, my back and bottom still burning. What hurts more than the fresh welts on my skin is the feeling that something is wrong with me. Soon I will come to know that the deep place I go in solitude is an asset, a survival tool, but tonight my imagination feels like an aberration. A terrible flaw.

I pull my doll under the covers. I call her Little One. She has long wavy dark hair and green eyes that open and close. Green eyes like my father's. She's a beautiful doll, my favorite possession. I whisper into her smooth porcelain ear.

"I wish I would die so he'd suffer for what he did to me," I say, my eyes clenched tight in the dark.

The Little One is quiet, as though considering this consuming anger I have at my father—and at myself. I let the fury churn in me. I whip it higher, steeper. There's pleasure in saying the worst possible things.

"No," I whisper to my doll, my voice ragged with tears, "I wish . . ." I let the crescendo build. . . . "I wish . . ." I will say it, the most violent and terrible thing I can think. A sentence so dreadful that I can't ever take it back, that I don't know yet will haunt me, will replay in my mind on far worse nights, at much darker times. "I wish my father was dead," I say.

Tonight the Little One says nothing, her eyes closed in the dark, a curtain pulled swiftly across the stage.

Chapter 2
SAFE IN OUR MINDS

Before World War I, the Slovakian region where I was born and raised was part of Austro-Hungary, a major empire and industrial power with Europe's second-largest railway system. But after World War I, in 1918, almost a decade before I was born, a new country was established: Czechoslovakia. My hometown—Kassa, Hungary—became Košice, Czechoslovakia. And my family became double minorities. We were ethnic Hungarians living in a predominately Czech country, and we were Jewish.

We weren't segregated. We weren't ghettoized—forced to live apart, as was common for Jews in many European countries (which is why my family spoke Hungarian exclusively and not Yiddish). We enjoyed plenty of educational, professional, and cultural opportunities. But we still encountered prejudice, both subtle and explicit. Anti-Semitism wasn't a Nazi invention—it existed long before the

Nazis. Growing up, I internalized the belief that it was safer to assimilate, to blend in, to never stand out.

But there were times in my childhood when I felt proud of who I was. In November 1938, when I was eleven, Hungary annexed Košice again, and it felt like home had become home. My mother stood on the balcony of our big apartment on the main street of our town, an old building called Andrássy Palace that had been carved into single-family apartments. Ours was on the third floor. My mother had draped an Oriental rug across the railing. She wasn't cleaning; she was celebrating. Admiral Miklós Horthy, His Serene Highness the Regent of the Kingdom of Hungary, would arrive that day to formally welcome our town into Hungary. I felt excited and proud. We belonged!

That afternoon I, too, welcomed Horthy. I performed a dance. I wore a Hungarian costume: bold floral embroidery on a bright wool vest and skirt, billowing white-sleeved blouse, ribbons, lace, red boots. When I did the high kick by the river, Horthy applauded. He embraced the dancers. He embraced me. I felt like an asset to my family and my country.

Yet that feeling of worth and belonging was temporary.

"Dicuka," Magda whispered to me that night at bedtime, "I wish we were blond like Klara." She meant that it's best not to let on that we're Jewish.

We were still years away from curfews and discriminatory laws, but Magda was right to be concerned. Horthy's parade was the starting point of all that would come.

Hungarian citizenship brought belonging in one sense but exclusion in another. We were so happy to speak our native tongue, to be accepted as Hungarians—but that acceptance depended on our assimilation. Neighbors argued that only ethnic Hungarians *who are not Jewish* should be allowed to wear the traditional garments.

Just a year after Horthy's parade, in 1939, the same year that Nazi Germany invaded Poland, the Hungarian Nazis—the *nyilas*—occupied the apartment below ours in Andrássy Palace. They spit at Magda. They evicted us. We moved to our current apartment, at Kossuth Lajos Utca #6, on a side street instead of the main road, less convenient for my father's business. The apartment was available because its former occupants, another Jewish family, had left for South America. We knew of other Jewish families leaving Hungary. My father's sister Matilda had been gone for years already, but her life in America seemed more circumscribed than ours. We didn't talk about leaving.

Then in 1940, the year I turn thirteen, the *nyilas* begin to round up the Jewish men of Kassa and send them to a forced labor camp. My father isn't taken. Not at first. But I hold my breath each day as I walk home from school. Will this be the day I come home to find my mother crying in the kitchen? Is this the day she'll tell me my father's gone? That I'll have to face the terrible consequence of my terrible wish? Is this the day we'll have to reckon with an insurmountable harm?

I'm scared, but the fear is more personal. It's more about something I feel I've done wrong. The war itself feels far away from us. If we don't pay attention, it seems we can continue our lives unnoticed. We can make the world safe in our minds. We can make ourselves invisible to harm.

We cultivate innocence. One day, I go home with my friend Sara after school, as is our custom—her mother greets us, puts a snack on the kitchen table, rye bread covered with butter and salami, steaming cocoa—and we devise a game. We will sashay up to boys at school or on the street. "Meet us at four o'clock by the clock on the square," we will trill, batting our eyelashes.

We are experimenting with our changing bodies, with raised stakes, with this new reality where boys and girls have crushes on each other and flirt. There's an enhanced sense of anticipation in everything. Who is looking at me? Who is noticing me? Where does this looking and noticing lead?

We sense these questions, but they aren't things we can put into words. There's so much we're ignorant of. When Sara's mom had a baby a few years before, I asked my mother where babies come from. "Your stomach opens up," she told me. I examined my stomach that night. I knew nothing of my anatomy. I guessed that my belly button must be the part that opened.

At thirteen, my body is still a mystery, yet there's something about the adult world, the dance of courtship, that Sara and I must intuitively understand, because our game works perfectly. Every time we sway our hips at boys and say meet us at the clock tower, the boys come. They always come, sometimes giddy, sometimes shy, sometimes swaggering with expectation. From the safety of my bedroom, Sara and I stand at the window and watch them arrive.

Sometimes we can't ignore the world around us. Sometimes the war punctures through. One day in June, Magda is out on her bicycle when the sirens roar. She dashes three blocks to the safety of our grandparents' house, only to find half of it gone. They survived, thank God. But their landlady didn't. It was a singular attack, one neighborhood razed by one bombing. We're told the Russians are responsible for the rubble and death. No one believes it, and yet no one can refute it. We are lucky and vulnerable in the same instant. The only solid truth is the pile of smashed brick in the spot where a house used to be. Destruction and absence—these become facts. Hungary joins Germany in Operation Barbarossa. We invade Russia.

Around this time, we are made to wear the yellow star. The trick is to hide the star, to let your sweater cover it. But even with my star out of sight, I feel like I have done something bad, something punishable. What is my unpardonable sin? My mother is always near the radio. When we picnic by the river, my father tells stories about being a prisoner of war in Russia during World War I. I know that his POW experience—his trauma, though I don't know to call it that—has something to do with his eating pork, with his distance from religion. I know that war is at the root of his distress. But the war, this war, is still elsewhere. I can ignore it, and I do.

Sara and I complete Jewish grade school and take a test to determine which high school we can attend. Many kids our age go to vocational school to learn trades. Magda has begun working with our father. She's a talented seamstress. I could also learn to sew. At the breakfast table, at the supper table, we speak of the latest news from Klara in Budapest, where she is studying at the conservatory, but we don't talk about my future. It's as though Klara's talent and ambitions are vast enough to carry everyone along on her back. I don't need wings of my own. Klara's will do.

What are my dreams for myself? They're more about now than about the future. In my gymnastics training, I learn to climb the rope, all the way up to the top of the room. I sway high above the other students and touch the ceiling. It's a powerful feeling, a summit. I have conquered storms and crossed through clouds, I imagine, to reach the top of the world.

I'm double-jointed, and there are many things I can do on the mat that the other girls can't do. I can walk on my hands. I can do a backbend and reach all the way back to touch my ankles with my fingers. It's not just that my body is flexible and strong—it's how I talk to myself on the mat, whether I tell myself I can or cannot do it. I say, "Yes I can." I give myself lots of yeses.

Sometimes I peel away from Sara after school, even though I love going to her house, the way her mother greets us like we belong, and I walk alone out to the suburbs where my gymnastics coach lives. I'm half in love with her. It's not a romantic crush. It's more like hero worship. When I reach her house, I pass by as slowly as possible, hoping to catch a glimpse of her through the window, fantasizing that she'll see me outside and invite me in. I'm curious about her life, about this version of adulthood, of womanhood. She isn't married. She isn't a mother. Her life is her profession. She's no-nonsense. In gymnastics, in athletics, you either do it, or you don't. You climb the rope, you land the flip, or you don't. She's a person who says, "Do it! Let's go." My sense of self and purpose and possibility rest within the scope of her support and faith in me. I feel that if I can manage to absorb all she has to teach me, and if I can fulfill her trust in me, then great things lie in store.

There's another facet to my obsession with her. To see something of her life outside of the studio is to learn something about my own life. There are alternatives to my mother's loneliness. I know there are.

Sara and I both pass the test and are accepted into the elite girls' high school in Kassa. Magda watches me dress for the first day of school. I put on the school uniform—a white blouse, navy blue pleated skirt, navy blue knee socks.

"Well, at least there won't be boys around to see your nothing chest," she teases.

I'm so accustomed to her brash way of speaking, her effortless beauty, her sophistication, that it has never occurred to me that she's jealous of me. I'm the runt of the family, the unwanted child, the one who keeps her parents company while her sisters wow the world with their talent and good looks. But for a moment I see a different version of the story, the one in which I am somebody, in which my oldest sister wishes she were me. This story is fleeting.

"I bet they'll pile on the homework," she says. "You'll become a shut-in, stuck behind a wall of books."

Maybe I will.

That's the thing about learning. You can know and know and know yet never reach the summit. Learning is a rope that never touches the ceiling. I want that kind of climb—a never-ending ascent, a life in the sky.

I settle into high school life, walking with Sara in the morning, then slipping into the sea of mostly non-Jewish girls, my priority always to fit in. To belong. I study German and Latin. I learn love songs in French. I read philosophy. My Latin teacher is my favorite. She tells us that learning Latin isn't just learning a language—it's learning how to think. *Tempora mutantur, nos et mutamur in illis*, we learn. Times are changing, and we are changing with the times. Maybe she's talking about the war without talking about the war. Or maybe she's touching on this time of life. Time churns on, transforming us. To be alive is to change.

I join a book club. Students from the nearby private boys' high school also attend. I feel awkward walking into the classroom for my first meeting. There's a different energy in the room. Should I look at the boys, or not? If I look, should I pretend I'm not looking? I watch the other girls for clues. Am I the only one wondering where I should put my eyes, how I should arrange myself in my chair?

I can't help looking. There's a redheaded boy across the room. He leans forward, eager, serious. His mind seems alive. My stomach flips when he speaks. I like the sound of his voice, masculine, thoughtful. I listen. I hold my body in absolute stillness. But I'm so alive on the inside, my whole being a mix of excited and calm. *Take another look*, says a voice within. *This one's special.*

As the weeks pass, I learn that the tall boy with reddish hair and freckles is named Eric. He plays soccer. In book club we read Stefan Zweig's *Marie Antoinette: The Portrait of an Average Woman.* We talk about Zweig's way of writing about history from the inside, from the mind of one person. I imagine Versailles. I imagine Marie Antoinette's boudoir. I imagine meeting Eric there. It makes me blush, I don't even know what to imagine happening between us, but I hear myself wonder, *What would our children look like? Would they have freckles too?* When he passes by my desk, he smells so good—like fresh air, like the grass on the banks of the Hornád River where my family goes on picnics.

Another week we read Sigmund Freud's *The Interpretation of Dreams.* Freud's idea of a dynamic unconscious life seems true to me. It makes sense that our inner lives are as alive as our outer ones—maybe more alive. I say so at our book club meeting, and sparks go off inside as I notice Eric noticing me. Our eyes meet, and it's as though a message is being passed between us. Some kind of recognition. *You too?* we seem to ask.

I'm inspired to talk to him after the meeting. My body propels me to his side of the room before I have a chance to change my mind. My mouth is speaking. I talk without a plan, off the cuff. I can hardly track what I'm saying to him—something about soccer. When does he practice, what position does he play. All I know is the feeling of the nearness of him, of his eyes and voice directed solely at me.

I take Sara with me to watch him play soccer after school one day. I can see from the way he carries himself on the field that he is good and kind. He's a strong player, assertive with the ball, but he doesn't go to extremes as some of the other boys do, acting out disappointment or frustration. He makes a pass to his teammate, who scores a goal, and Eric smiles, cheering the other boy on.

"I like him," Sara says. She doesn't go giddy and silly over my crush. She takes me seriously. As much as I tell myself it doesn't matter what she thinks of him, it does matter, and I'm glad she approves.

"Just don't go to bed with him," Magda warns when she's finally wrested from me the private detail that there's a boy I like.

I don't know what she means, not exactly. In our small apartment, it's difficult sometimes not to catch a glimpse of our parents in bed. I have no details about their private business. It makes me uncomfortable to think of it, yet when Magda tells me not to go to bed with Eric, I feel that it's something I want. How is it possible to want something when you don't know what it is? Yet I do.

Eric starts walking me home from school, carrying my books. He tells me he wants to be a doctor. He's voracious and curious, but he wants to pursue knowledge not just for the sake of knowledge, but to help people. I tell him I plan to be a teacher.

"What will you teach?" he asks. He wants to know. He also says it with admiration, as though he believes there are many subjects that I could teach well.

"Philosophy," I tell him, and he smiles. I like that he's pleased. I feel that he's proud of me. I'm used to holding my strengths and assets alone. My parents don't come to watch my gymnastics competitions. Klara is the special one, the celebrated one. It just isn't my role in the family. And so my successes are as private as my yearnings and disappointments. But here is a person who sees who I am and wish to be and smiles.

"Editke," he says one afternoon as we walk the main street toward my apartment.

My body flushes at the term of endearment. It's heavenly to hear him say my name—Edith—but even better to hear him add the "ke." *Editke. Little Edith.* As though I'm a treasure.

"Editke," he says again. "There's an American jazz band playing on Saturday. Would you like to go hear them play? With me?" His cheeks have gone pink. His hair is gold in the sun.

"I'll ask my parents," I say. I feel sheepish. Bells are ringing in my chest, but I can't say yes without permission.

My mother is stirring a pot of chicken broth when I get home, the kitchen steamy, smelling of garlic and the richness of bone marrow.

I speak the words fast, as though my request is unremarkable, as though I'm not bursting with longing and surprise. I've been asked on a date! To hear music! To dance! He asked *me*.

My mother stirs the pot slowly, savory steam rising in her face. "Ah," she says. I catch something like a smile on her face. "He's a nice boy, Dicuka?"

"Yes, Mama," I say. I'm not sure why tears are forming in my eyes. It's something about my mother's almost-smile, about the happiness I see she wants for me.

"Your father and I will be happy to meet him," she says.

On Saturday I put on a white pleated skirt. I realize Eric has only seen me in my school uniform. I feel a little vulnerable. Will he like me in the clothes I've chosen? I dab cologne behind my ears. It's my own cologne that my mother allowed me to purchase with my own money. Sometimes she uses it too. It smells like anticipation. Like an orchestra tuning up.

I barely eat supper. Eric rings the doorbell just as my mother has cleared away the plates. My father brings his cigarette into the parlor, which is also the place where he sees customers, and offers Eric a seat. I can hear the worry start up in my mind, the wondering whether things will be stiff and awkward, whether something will go wrong, but what I actually feel in the room is kindness. My parents are ready to like Eric. They're not poised to critique or reject him. This thing I've never done before—brought a boy home to introduce to them—isn't such a big deal.

Eric takes my hand on the walk to the restaurant where the band will play. It's not yet night. His hand feels like I knew it would feel. Familiar. Warm.

At the restaurant, he orders us cocoa. We are the youngest people in the room. The music is bright. Jubilant. It's music from across the ocean, where the war is even farther away. I imagine we're in New York, Hitler nothing but a name on a scrap of newspaper blown along a city street, a name you can't see in the dark.

"Shall we dance?" Eric asks, standing up from our tiny table set against the wall. I take his hand, and we move to the open floor. I've danced with my father, standing on his feet, and I've danced in performances, but I've never danced with my face inches from a chest I'd like to lean on, my hand on a shoulder I suddenly realize I'd like to see bare. Eric's a good dancer, confident, moving in time, certain where he's leading us, and I relax into the rhythm of the beat, of our bodies stepping toward and apart and around. He twirls me, my skirt spinning wide, and pulls me back, pulls me close to his body. I feel a spark between us, a desire, sharp and sweet inside, as I press against him, as I feel a part of him I've never seen reaching toward me, come to life.

Chapter 3

LOVE AND WAR

Our relationship holds weight and substance from the start. We talk about literature, history, and philosophy. This isn't a time of carefree dating. Our bond isn't a casual crush, a puppy love. This is love in the face of war. A curfew has been imposed on Jews, but we sneak out for a walk one early summer night without wearing our yellow stars.

"Editke," Eric murmurs when we reach my apartment. He hugs me close. I rest my cheek on his chest. I close my eyes. I can almost feel the war brewing around us, a subtle vibration, the way the ground shakes in advance of a train. But it's far away. We never know what is coming next. Eric's heartbeat pulses against my face. The way we are touching—this is real. This is here and now. Maybe we're lucky to be falling in love at this moment. Maybe the turmoil around us gives us the opportunity for more commitment, less questioning.

Eric loosens his embrace and takes my hands. "We could leave," he says.

"Leave Kassa?"

"Leave Hungary," he says. "Leave Europe. Hitler will soon be everywhere."

"And go where?" I ask. I think of my aunt Matilda in New York, of my mother's reluctance to send Klara to study there.

"Palestine," Eric says. "We could help create a safe place for our people. A Jewish homeland."

This isn't the first time I've been exposed to Zionist ideals, but it's the first time I've thought about it in a personal way. I try to picture our lives in a desert. Would we live in a tent? In rugged mountains? Would our families come with us?

"We could leave, just the two of us," he says.

"And our future?"

"We'd get settled there. Then I'd get my medical degree. You could teach. We could raise our children in a safe place. No Hitler or yellow stars."

It's the first time he's mentioned having a family with me. It feels romantic—and yet it's the war on his mind as much as it's me. And we're so young. I'm not yet sixteen.

He squeezes my hands.

"Don't do anything you don't want to do," he says. "It's important to be sure."

My mouth feels dry. Would he go without me?

Or, more terrifying, might I leave my family? Is this really what we're discussing? Leaving my father's charming smile and chalk-covered hands, leaving my mother's warm kitchen? Leaving family picnics, the bus to the countryside, the walk up the mountainside, the meal enjoyed on a blanket on the ground, fried chicken and potato salad? Leaving Magda's saucy laugh, the way she twinkles her eyes and shakes her head, the way she says, "Take it, I'll eat it"? Leaving my ballet and gymnastics studios, the thriving I feel as my body climbs the rope?

I lie awake most of the night pondering the question Eric has put before me.

My mother takes Sara and me cherry-picking at a wealthy classmate's house in the country, and I ask Sara what she thinks I should do. She listens carefully, her fingers tugging the ripe fruit. Sara isn't conventionally beautiful, but she is beautiful to me—bathed in sunlight, lips stained with cherry juice, her presence loyal, steady.

"You have doubt?" she says. She speaks it like a question, but I understand that she's holding up a mirror where I can take a clear look at myself; she's telling me what she hears in my voice.

I want to be that certain. Committed. Sure.

"What does your gut say?" Sara asks.

How can I listen to what I *really* feel? Not to the part that *wants* to feel a certain way? My head pounds with what-ifs. What if I go and I miss my family? What if I go and never see them again? What if I go and end up lonely and friendless? What if I go and Eric falls in love with someone else?

"I don't feel ready," I say. "I don't feel ready to leave for the unknown."

Eric doesn't pressure me. As summer moves toward fall, he still talks about Palestine, but it's a vague idea about the future. It's not a real plan. Sometimes I go along with the fantasy and imagine a life there. Sometimes I tell him I'm not sure. Sometimes I push the question out of my mind. Sometimes I convince myself that no one else knows what will come to pass, but we do. We have each other and the future, a life together we can see as clearly as we can see our hands when we join them.

We go to the river one August day in 1943. He brings a camera—his father is a lawyer and can afford such luxuries—and photographs me in my bathing suit, doing the splits in the grass. I imagine showing our children the picture one day. Telling them how we held our love and our commitment bright.

But when I come home that day, my father is gone.

"He was taken" is all my mother will say.

She means to the forced labor camp, where other Jewish men have been sent.

"He's a tailor," I protest. "He's apolitical!" But my indignation is a shield. If I can protest the illogic of his imprisonment, then I don't have to accept that it has happened. My rage and righteousness distance me from the agonizing truth. In a way, so does my guilt. I can't stop thinking of the night two years ago when my father beat me, and I wished him dead. I press on my regret like a bruise. It's irrational to think I caused my father's punishment, his disappearance. Yet if I cling to the guilt, then I don't have to grieve. I can turn the sorrow on myself. I can think about how flawed I am instead of feeling the terrible ache. Or maybe the guilt is just a way of trying to stay in control. If I caused it, then there is a cause, and the world lines up in the expected way.

My mother just looks at me sadly. "I sent word to Klara," she says.

Suddenly, I'm angry. Not at the *nyilas.* I'm angry at my mother, at her wishful thinking, at the part of her that stores every hope in Klara. Klara knows famous musicians and composers. She'll help us somehow. But Klarie is just a girl with a violin. A girl who will worry, who will feel responsible for us. Who might drop her life at the conservatory to help us, and I don't want any of it. Why are Magda and I not enough to comfort our mother, to give her strength? Why is she so quick to despair? Why won't she comfort me?

School resumes. Sara's and Eric's fathers are still at home. My father's imprisonment drags on.

My mother won't speak her fears out loud, but I see her trying to make several meals out of one chicken. She gets migraines. We take in a boarder to make up for the loss of income. He owns a store across the street from our apartment, and I sit long hours in his store just to be near his comforting presence.

Magda, who is essentially an adult now, finds out somehow where our father is and visits him. She watches him stagger under the weight of a table he has to heft from place to place. This is the only detail she tells me of her visit. I don't know what this image means. I don't know what work it is that my father is forced to do in his captivity. I don't know how long he will be a prisoner. I have two images of my father: one, as I have known him my entire life, cigarette hanging out of his mouth, tape measure around his neck, chalk in his hand for marking a pattern onto expensive cloth, his eyes twinkling, ready to burst into song, about to tell a joke. And this new one: lifting a table that is too heavy, in a no-name place, a no-man's-land.

When I tell Eric this news about my father, he broaches again the conversation about Palestine.

"Have you thought more about leaving?" he asks.

Of course I have. Yet while my father's imprisonment makes the possibility of leaving more urgent, it also makes it impossible. I could never abandon my family, I could never leave without saying goodbye to my father.

"Why do you think he was targeted?" I ask Eric. I am still trying to find a reason, to forge order and logic from something that doesn't make sense. I want to manage my helplessness with questions that have answers.

"It's a power play," Eric replies. "They took him because they could. Because it shows their strength and menace."

My father has survived such trials before. He was a POW in the Great War. He'll know what to do, how to manage, how to survive. This is how I comfort myself.

In late September, on my sixteenth birthday, I stay home from school with a cold, and Eric comes to our apartment to deliver sixteen roses. It's the most romantic gesture I've ever received. I bury my face in the flowers, my head too congested to really smell them, but I relish the feel of the soft petals on my face. Eric takes the roses from me, sets them on a side table, and pulls me into his chest. I lean into his sweet sturdiness. He takes my shoulders and moves me away from him so he can look in my eyes. Then his lips move toward mine, and I close my eyes to receive his sweet kiss.

I am happy, but I am sad too. What can I hold on to? What lasts?

The next day, I give the picture Eric took of me on the riverbank to a friend. I can't remember why. For safekeeping? Somehow I must have known that I would need someone to preserve evidence of my life, that I would need to plant proof of myself around me like seeds.

Eric and I spend the winter sneaking out past curfew, standing in line at the cinema, finding our seats in the dark. We see an American film, starring Bette Davis. *Now, Voyager*, I later learn, is its American name, but in Hungary it's called *Utazás a múltból*, Journey to the Past. Bette Davis plays an unmarried daughter tyrannized by her controlling mother. She tries to find herself and her freedom but is constantly knocked down by her mother's criticisms.

"It's a metaphor," Eric says on our walk home to my family's apartment. "A political message. If Nazi Germany is the mother, Hungary and other European countries are like the daughter trying to gain self-determination."

I see his point. Yet for me the film is more personal; it's about self-worth. In the mother and daughter, I see shades of my mother and Magda—my mother, who adores Eric but chastises Magda for her casual dating; who begs me to eat more but refuses to fill Magda's plate; who is often silent and introspective but rages at Magda; whose anger, though it is never directed at me, terrifies me all the same.

Another night we see *For Whom the Bell Tolls*, about an American fighting in the Spanish Civil War who falls in love with a female guerrilla fighter. The violence in the film is shocking to me—and thrilling. It's a relief to see conflict made physical. To see an uprising against fascism. To see that something can be done. Gary Cooper's character, Roberto, clings to the underside of a bridge, laying a bomb to disrupt a line of tanks, and I sit forward in my seat, squeezing Eric's hand in the dark theater, my heart racing. A man, one singular body, against a procession of military machines.

It's not just a war story, though. It's a love story. Ingrid Bergman's character, Maria, is a fighter too, her hair cut short like a boy's. She wears a green button-down shirt tucked into blue, belted dungarees. She rakes her fingers through her short curls. "This is how I comb it," she says. Sexy. Confident. She's strong and bright, yet a deep, forever sorrow lies just below the surface. We learn she was a prisoner, tied by her wrists in a long line of women and girls, forced to watch her parents shot in front of her. She wanted to be shot too, to say, "Long live the Republic and my mother and father," and die, but she was given a different fate, something Roberto won't let her put into words, something terrible she only speaks with her eyes. One of the men tells Roberto that when Maria was rescued by the guerrilla group, her head had been shaved. "She looked like a half-drowned kitten," he says. "She's a very strange woman," he later adds. "She belongs to no one."

I'm fascinated by Maria—her luminous eyes and sprite-like grace, her fierce unbelonging and survival skills, and yet, despite all the ways she's lost and been harmed, her ready capacity for love. The way she quickens to it. Not with my sister's sultry sexiness. It's a different quality that makes her shine, an arresting genuineness. She's never pretending.

"I do not know how to kiss," she tells Roberto, "or I would kiss you. Where do the noses go?"

Their first kiss is so passionate, my stomach drops and swirls. I feel Eric's body next to mine, warm, his eyes focused on the screen.

Walking home, he is quiet, serious. "We don't know what's going to happen," he says.

"No," I agree. Did Maria feel safe before her village was taken by the enemy? Was she oblivious to the threat or aware of its imminence? What were the last words she said to her parents before they died?

"A man fights for what he believes in," he says. He's quoting Roberto from the movie.

"Whatever happens to you will happen to me," I reply. I'm echoing something Maria says to Roberto.

I think about the title of the film, *For Whom the Bell Tolls*. It comes from Ernest Hemingway's famous novel, but Hemingway took the words from John Donne: *Any man's death diminishes me, because I am involved in Mankind; And therefore never send to know for whom the bell tolls; it tolls for thee.* We're all interconnected, all humankind. We belong to each other. If you suffer, I suffer. If you die, I die. Our fates are intertwined. War makes this obvious. We are all subject to the same fears, harshness, deprivations. Yet to be "involved in Mankind" is also to be baffled by choices. To feel lost in the vastness. To struggle to find direction, to struggle to choose.

I think of Maria, so confident and unwavering in her love. "I love you, Roberto," she says. "Always remember. I love you as I loved my father and mother, as I love our unborn children, as I love what I love most in the world, and I love you more. Always remember."

Chapter 4
THE FOUR QUESTIONS

The weather slowly warms. My father is still gone. No letters. No news. My mother's fear and despair cast a heavy shadow on our home. Yet we never cry together.

I ride my bike home from my grandparents' house one day. I'm wearing the white pleated skirt I wore on my first date with Eric. When I get home, I see blood streaks all over my white skirt. I'm frightened. I run to my mother, I'm crying. I need her to help me locate the wound. She slaps me. It's a Hungarian tradition for a girl to be slapped upon her first period, but I don't know about menstruation at all. I know my body well enough to propel it into the air, to bend backward into a wheel, yet I know nothing of my cycles, anatomy, womanhood.

"Don't get knocked up," Magda says. I hear a warning behind her teasing voice. The stakes are high. Even my own body could betray me.

In March, seven months after my father's imprisonment, I come home from school to find him sitting with my mother at the kitchen table.

"Papa!" I cry. I run into his arms. He pulls me into his lap, as though I am a little girl, and nuzzles the back of my head with his nose. Life restored.

Yet the questions press. "What did they make you do?" I ask. "Will they take you again?"

"Dicuka," my mother scolds. "He's home, and we're grateful. Let him rest."

"Ilonka," my father says, "she's not a child."

He lifts me up from his lap, motions for me to sit at the table across from him, and asks my mother to warm some cocoa for me to drink. He lights a cigarette. His hands are chapped and rough; his fingers look stiff.

"There are things I'll never tell you," he says. "They are my burden. I will carry the memories alone. I will not make you hold them." His voice cracks. He drags on the cigarette and exhales, smoke mingling with the steam from my cup. "I will tell you, though, that there were times I felt so desperate, when life seemed so futile, that I wanted to die."

My mother draws her breath in sharply. She gives him a warning glance.

"Stop," my father tells her. He turns back to face me. "Dicuka," he says, "there's a war raging. The threat of death is all around. It's tempting to give up. I'm telling you now, and I'll never speak of it again, that I urge you, I beg you, when things take a bad turn"—tears fall freely down his stubbled cheeks—"choose life."

Then he puts out his cigarette and stands up. "I'm heading out for a short while," he says. I assume he means to see his friends, his billiards cronies, to tell them he's returned, maybe to win a few coins, share some laughs. It doesn't occur to me that there's anyone else he might be anxious to see, any other reason for my mother to lower her head quickly, but not before I see her wince.

I sit on the blue mat in the gymnastics studio one day, a few weeks after my father's return, warming up with a floor routine, pointing my toes, flexing my feet, lengthening my legs and arms and neck and back. I feel like myself again. I'm not the little cross-eyed runt afraid to speak her name. I'm not the daughter afraid for her family. I am an artist and an athlete, my body strong and limber. I don't have Magda's looks or Klara's fame, but I have my lithe and expressive body, the budding existence of which is the only true thing I need. My training, my skill—my life brims with possibility. The best of us in my gymnastics class have formed an Olympic training team. The 1944 Olympics have been canceled due to the war, but that just gives us more time to prepare to compete.

I close my eyes and stretch my arms and torso forward across my legs. My friend nudges me with her toe, and I lift my head to see our coach walking straight toward me, the coach whose neighborhood I visit, whose home I try to gaze inside. The coach I practically worship.

"Editke," she says as she approaches my mat. "A word, please."

Her fingers glide once over my back as she ushers me into the hall.

I look at her expectantly. Maybe she has noticed my improvements on the vault. Maybe she would like me to lead the team in more stretching exercises at the end of practice today. Maybe she wants to invite me over for supper. I'm ready to say yes before she has even asked.

"I don't know how to tell you this," she begins. She studies my face and then looks away toward the window, where the dropping sun blazes in.

"Is it my sister?" I ask before I even realize the terrible picture forming in my mind. My mother has gone to Budapest to see Klara perform a concert and to fetch her home for Passover, and as my coach stands awkwardly beside me in the hall, unable to meet my eyes, I worry that their train has derailed. It's too early in the week for them to be traveling home, but that is the only tragedy I can think of. Even in a time of war, the first disaster to cross my mind is a mechanical one, a tragedy of human error, not of human design, although I am aware that some of Klara's teachers, including some of the gentile ones, have already fled Europe because they fear what is to come.

"Your family is fine." Her tone doesn't reassure me. "Edith. This isn't my choice. But I must be the one to tell you that your place on the Olympic training team will go to someone else."

I think I might vomit. I feel foreign in my own skin. "What did I do?" I comb over the rigorous months of training for the thing I've done wrong. "I don't understand."

"My child," she says, and now she looks me full in the face, which is worse, because I can see that she is crying, and at this moment, when my dreams are being shredded like newspaper at the butcher shop, I do not want to feel pity for her. "The simple truth is that because of your background, you are no longer qualified."

I think of the kids who've spit at me and called me a dirty Jew, of Jewish friends who have stopped going to school to avoid harassment and now get their courses over the radio. "If someone spits at you, spit back," my father has instructed me. "That's what you do." I consider spitting on my coach. But to fight back would be to accept her devastating news. I won't accept it.

"I'm not Jewish," I say.

"I'm sorry, Editke," she says. "I'm so sorry. I still want you at the studio. I would like to ask you to train the girl who will replace you on the team." Again, her fingers are on my back. In another year, my back will be broken in exactly the spot she now caresses. Within weeks, my very life will be on the line. But here in the hallway of my cherished studio, my life feels like it is already over.

In the days that follow my expulsion from the Olympic training team, I don't tell anyone what has happened, not even my family or Eric. I don't want to worry or burden them. Instead, I plot my revenge. It won't be the revenge of hate; it will be the revenge of perfection. I will show my coach that I am the best. The most accomplished athlete. The best trainer. I will train my replacement so meticulously that I will prove what a mistake has been made by cutting me from the team. On the day that my mother and Klara are due back from Budapest, I cartwheel my way down the red-carpeted hall toward our apartment, imagining my replacement as my understudy, myself the headlining star.

My mother and Magda are in the kitchen. Magda's chopping apples for the charoset. My mother is stirring matzo meal. They glower over their work, barely registering my arrival. This is their relationship now. They fight all the time, and when they're not fighting, they treat each other as though they are already in a face-off. Their arguments used to be about food, my mother always concerned about Magda's weight. But now the conflict has grown to a general and chronic hostility. "Where's Klarie?" I ask, swiping chopped walnuts from a bowl.

"Budapest," Magda says. My mother slams her bowl onto the counter. I want to ask why my sister isn't with us for the holiday. Has she really chosen music over us? Or was she not allowed to miss class for a holiday that none of her fellow students celebrates? But I don't ask. I am afraid my questions will bring my mother's obviously simmering anger to a boil. I retreat to the bedroom we all share, my parents, Magda, and me.

On any other evening, especially a holiday, we would gather around the piano, the instrument Magda had been playing and studying since she was young, where Magda and my father would take turns leading us in songs. Magda and I weren't prodigies like Klara, but we still had creative passions that our parents recognized and nurtured. After Magda played, it would be my turn to perform. "Dance, Dicuka!" my mother would say. And even though it was more a demand than an invitation, I'd savor my parents' attention and praise. Then Klara, the star attraction, would play her violin, and my mother would look transformed. But there is no music in our house tonight.

Before the meal, Magda tries to cheer me up by reminding me of seders past, when I would stuff socks in my bra to impress Klara, wanting to show her that I'd become a woman while she was away. "Now you've got your own womanhood to flaunt around," Magda says. At the seder table, she continues the antics, splashing her fingers around in the glass of wine we've set for Prophet Elijah, as is the custom. Elijah, who saves Jews from peril. On any other night, our father might laugh, despite himself. On any other night, our mother would end the silliness with a stern rebuke. But tonight our father is too distracted to notice, and our mother is too distraught by Klara's absence to chastise Magda. When we open the apartment door to let the prophet in, I feel a chill that has nothing to do with the cool evening. In some deep part of myself, I know how badly we need protection now.

"You tried the consulate?" my father asks. He isn't even pretending to lead the seder anymore. No one but Magda can eat. "Ilona?"

"I tried the consulate," my mother says. It is as though she conducts her part in the conversation from another room.

"Tell me again what Klara said."

"Again?" my mother protests.

"Again."

She tells it blankly, her fingers fidgeting with her napkin. Klara had called her hotel at four that morning. Klara's professor had just told her that a former professor at the conservatory, Béla Bartók, now a famous composer, had called from America with a warning: The Germans in Czechoslovakia and Hungary were going to start closing their fist; Jews would be taken away come morning. Klara's professor forbade her to return home to Kassa. He wanted her to urge my mother to stay in Budapest as well and send for the rest of the family.

"Ilona, why did you come home?" my father moans.

My mother stabs her eyes at him. "What about all that we've worked for here? We should just leave it? And if you three couldn't make it to Budapest? You want me to live with that?"

I don't realize that they are terrified. I hear only the blame and disappointment that my parents routinely pass between them like the mindless shuttle on a loom. *Here's what you did. Here's what you didn't do. Here's what you did. Here's what you didn't do.* Later I'll learn that this isn't just their usual quarreling, that there's a history and a weight to the dispute they are having now. There are the tickets to America my father turned away. There is the Hungarian official who approached my mother with fake papers for the whole family, urging us to flee. Later we learn that they both had a chance to choose differently. Now they suffer with their regret, and they cover their regret with blame.

"Can we do the four questions?" I ask to disrupt my parents' gloom. That is my job in the family. To play peacemaker between my parents, between Magda and my mother. Whatever plans are being made outside our door, I can't control. But inside our home, I have a role to fill. It is my job as the youngest child to ask the four questions. I don't even have to open my Haggadah. I know the text by heart. "Why is this night different from all other nights?" I begin.

At the end of the meal, my father circles the table, kissing each of us on the head. He's crying. *Why is this night different from all other nights?* Before dawn breaks, we'll know.

Chapter 5

WHAT YOU PUT IN YOUR MIND

They come in the dark. They pound on the door; they yell. Does my father let them in, or do they force their way into our apartment? Are they German soldiers, or *nyilas*? I can't make sense out of the noises that startle me from sleep. My mouth still tastes of seder wine. The soldiers storm into the bedroom, announcing that we're being moved from our home and resettled somewhere else. We're allowed one suitcase for all four of us. I can't seem to find my legs to get off the cot where I sleep at the foot of my parents' bed, but my mother is instantly in motion. Before I know it, she is dressed and reaching high into the closet for the little box that I know holds Klara's caul, the piece of amniotic sac that covered her head and face like a helmet when she was born. Midwives used to save cauls and sell them to sailors as protection against drowning. My mother doesn't trust the box to the suitcase—she tucks it deep into the pocket of her coat, a good luck totem. I don't know if my mother packs the caul to protect Klara, or all of us.

"Hurry, Dicu," she urges me. "Get up. Get dressed."

"Not that wearing clothes ever did your figure any good," Magda whispers. There's no reprieve from her teasing. How will I know when it's time to be really afraid?

My mother is in the kitchen now, packing leftover food, pots, and pans. In fact, she will keep us alive for two weeks on the supplies she thinks to carry with us now—some flour, some chicken fat. My father paces the bedroom and living room, picking up books, candlesticks, clothing, putting things down. "Get blankets," my mother calls to him. I think that if he had one petit four, that is the thing he would take along, if only for the joy of handing it to me later, of seeing a swift second of delight on my face. Thank goodness my mother is more practical. When she was still a child, she became a mother to her younger siblings, and she staved their hunger through many seasons of grief. *As God is my witness*, I imagine her thinking now, as she packs, *I'm never going to be hungry again.* And yet I want her to drop the dishes, the survival tools, and come back to the bedroom to help me dress. Or at least I want her to call to me. To tell me what to wear. To tell me not to worry. To tell me all is well.

The soldiers stomp their boots and knock chairs over with their guns. *Hurry. Hurry.* I feel a sudden anger with my mother. She would save Klara before she would save me. She'd rather cull the pantry than hold my hand in the dark. I'll have to find my own sweetness, my own luck. Despite the chill of the dark April morning,

I put on a thin blue silk dress, the one I wore on my birthday, when Eric kissed me. I trace the pleats with my fingers. I fasten the narrow blue suede belt. I will wear this dress so that his arms can once again encircle me. This dress will keep me desirable, protected, ready to reclaim love. If I shiver, it will be a badge of hope, a signal of my trust in something deeper, better. I picture Eric and his family also dressing and scrambling in the dark. I can feel him thinking of me. A current of energy shoots down from my ears to my toes. I close my eyes and cup my elbows with my hands, allowing the afterglow of that flash of love and hope to keep me warm.

But the ugly present intrudes on my private world. "Where are the bathrooms?" one of the soldiers shouts at Magda. My bossy, sarcastic, flirtatious sister cowers under his glare. I've never known her to be afraid. She's never spared an opportunity to get a rise out of someone, to make people laugh. Authority figures have never held any power over her. In school she wouldn't stand up, as required, when a teacher entered the room. "Elefánt," her math teacher, a very short man, reprimanded her one day, calling her by our last name. My sister got up on tiptoes and peered at him. "Oh, are you there?" she said. "I didn't see you." But today the men hold guns. She gives no crude remark, no rebellious comeback. She points meekly down the hall toward the bathroom door. The soldier shoves her out of his way. He holds a gun. What other proof of his dominance does he need? This is when I start to see that it can always be so much worse. That every moment harbors a potential for violence. We never know when or how we will break. Doing what you're told might not save you.

"Out. Now. Time for you to take a little trip," the soldiers say. My mother closes the suitcase and my father lifts it. She fastens her gray coat and is the first to follow the commanding officer out into the street. I'm next, then Magda. Before we reach the wagon that sits ready for us at the curb, I turn to watch our father leave our home. He stands facing the door, suitcase in his hand, looking muddled, a midnight traveler patting down his pockets for his keys. A soldier yells a jagged insult and kicks our door back open with his heel.

"Go ahead," he says. "Take a last look. Feast your eyes."

My father gazes at the dark space. For a moment he seems confused, as though he can't determine whether the soldier has been generous or unkind. Then the soldier kicks him in the knee and my father hobbles toward us, toward the wagon where the other families wait.

I'm caught between the urge to protect my parents and the sorrow that they can no longer protect me. *Eric,* I pray, *wherever we are going, help me find you. Don't forget our future. Don't forget our love.* Magda doesn't say a word as we sit side by side on the bare board seats. In my catalog of regrets, this one shines bright: that I didn't reach for my sister's hand.

Just as daylight breaks, the wagon pulls up alongside the Jakab's brick factory at the edge of town, and we are herded inside. We are the lucky ones; early arrivers get quarters in the drying sheds. Most of the nearly twelve thousand Jews who will be imprisoned here will sleep without a roof over their heads. All of us will sleep on the floor. We will cover ourselves with our coats and shiver through the spring chill. We will cover our ears when, for minor offenses, people are beaten with rubber truncheons at the center of the camp. There is no running water here. Buckets come, never enough of them, on horse-drawn carts. At first the rations, combined with the pancakes my mother makes from the scraps she brought from home, are enough to feed us, but after only a few days, the hunger pains become a constant cramping throb. Magda sees her old gym teacher in the barracks next door, struggling to take care of a newborn baby in these starvation conditions. "What will I do when my milk is gone?" she moans to us. "My baby just cries and cries."

There are two sides to the camp, on either side of a street. Our side is occupied by the Jews from our section of town. We learn that all of Kassa's Jews are being held here at the brick factory. We find our neighbors, our shopkeepers, our teachers, our friends. But my grandparents, whose home was a thirty-minute walk from our apartment, are not on our side of the camp. Gates and guards separate us from the other side. We are not supposed to cross over. But I plead with a guard, and he says I can go in search of my grandparents. I walk the wall-less barracks, quietly repeating their names. As I pace up and down the rows of huddled families, I say Eric's name too. I tell myself that it is only a matter of time and perseverance. I will find him, or he will find me.

I don't find my grandparents. I don't find Eric. I think about things that don't matter and yet do: my doll, my Little One, left behind on my bed. A doll would do us no real good in this place.

Of all the things we had to leave behind, better to wish for food, blankets, things we could use. But my lonely left-behind doll bothers me. I hope another child gets her, holds her tight, watches her green eyes blink open.

One afternoon when the water carts arrive and the crowds rush to scoop a little pail of it, Eric spies me sitting alone, guarding my family's coats. He kisses my forehead, my cheeks, my lips. I touch the suede belt of my silk dress, praising it for its good luck.

We manage to meet every day after that. Sometimes we speculate about what will befall us. Rumors spread that we will be sent to a place called Kenyérmező, an internment camp, where we will work and live out the war with our families. We don't know that the rumor was started by the Hungarian police and *nyilas* dishing out false hope. After the war, piles of letters from concerned relatives in faraway cities will sit in stacks in post offices, unopened; the address lines read: *Kenyérmező*. No such place exists.

"Palestine," Eric says. Before the brick factory, this word filled me with sadness and dread. An impossible choice. Now it's a hopeful word. It means we are thinking beyond the present circumstances, that we can conjure a reality after the war. "If we can get to Vienna," he says, "then we can register for a transport to Palestine."

"Yes," I say. I urge him to keep talking, keep planning. I want to be with him, I want to imagine our future life together. If something worse is coming, I don't want to know.

From inside the brick factory we can hear the streetcars trundle past. They are within reach. How easy it could be to jump aboard.

But anyone who comes close to the outer fence is shot without warning. A girl only a little older than me tries to run. They hang her body in the middle of the camp as an example. My parents don't say a word to me or Magda about her death. "Try to get a little block of sugar," my father tells us. "Get a block of sugar and hold on to it. Always keep a little something sweet in your pocket." One day we hear that my grandparents have been sent away in one of the first transports to leave the factory. We'll see them in Kenyérmező, we think. I kiss Eric good night and trust that his lips are the sweetness I can count on.

One early morning, after we have been in the factory for about a month, our section of the camp is evacuated. I scramble to find someone who can pass a message to Eric. "Let it go, Dicu," my mother says. She and my father have written a goodbye letter to Klara, but there is no way to send it. I watch my mother throw it away, see her drop it onto the pavement like ash from a cigarette, see it disappear under three thousand pairs of feet. The silk of my dress brushes against my legs as we surge and stop and surge and stop, three thousand of us marched toward the factory gates, pressed into a long row of waiting trucks. Again we huddle in the dark. I wonder if Eric got the message, if he knows that we're being evacuated, if and when I'll see him again. Suddenly, I hear my name. It's Eric. He's calling through the slats of the truck. I shove my way toward his voice.

"I'm here!" I call as the engine starts. The slats are almost too narrow for me to see him. He comes right up to the truck, his hands pressed against the wooden boards that separate us.

"Editke," he says, "I ran to every truck, calling your name."

"You found me," I say. I try to push my fingers into the tiny cracks between the slats, but my fingertips can't reach him.

"We were put together for life," he says.

Others in the truck are also speaking through the boards. I can't see much outside, but I imagine others up and down the row of trucks, speaking sacred words.

"God chose that we'd meet," I say. "God brought us together to be with each other. We'll never part. We'll be together as long as we live."

Guards are yelling now, forcing everyone outside back inside the gates of the brick factory.

"I'll never forget your eyes," Eric says. "I'll never forget your hands."

His hands pull away from the slats. My fingertips feel nothing but cool air.

"Eric," I murmur. I imagine him beside me in the dark truck, how I'd lean into the crook of his arm, his fresh-grass smell.

I sit again with my family. No one speaks. My mother sits very straight. *I'll never forget your eyes. I'll never forget your hands.* I repeat Eric's words ceaselessly as the truck begins to move. We drive a short distance and stop again.

A guard bangs on the back of the truck. "Bathroom?" he yells. "Bathroom break."

"Yes!" I cry.

"Dicu!" my mother says. I've broken ranks.

I stand up and pick my way to the back of the truck. I'm surprised by my own actions, as though my body is moving all by itself, unmoored from my mind. The guard opens the door at the back, and I jump down. The sunlight is bright after the dark of the truck, but I can see that we're at a train station. The guard points down the platform, toward the bathrooms.

"Good to go now," he says, "but move fast. It's going to be a long trip."

Does he mean to intimidate me, or express an odd kind of care? I hurry toward the bathroom. What would happen if I ran back to the brick factory? Looked for Eric? I see someone I recognize pacing the platform—one of our neighbors, a gentile. He works at the train station. He sees me and waves. I could ask him for help. I could ask his family to take me home, to hide me. But my mother would worry. I picture her sitting tensely in the truck, her face and shoulders tightening with every minute I'm gone. I finish using the bathroom and run back to the truck. I sit down next to my mother. She sighs deeply.

Soon the truck door opens, and we're told to get out and board a crowded train car. I find that I can barely hear the shouting officers or crying children over the salve of Eric's remembered voice. *If I survive today,* I tell myself, *then I can show him my eyes. I can show him my hands.* I breathe to the rhythm of this chant. *If I survive today . . . If I survive today, tomorrow I'll be free.*

The train car is like none I've ever been in. It's not a passenger train; it's for transporting livestock or freight. We are human cargo. There are a hundred of us in one car. Each hour feels like a week. The uncertainty makes the moments stretch. The uncertainty and the relentless noise of the wheels on the track. There is one loaf of bread for eight people to share. One bucket of water. One bucket for our bodily waste. It smells of sweat and excrement. People die on the way. We all sleep upright, leaning against our family members, shouldering aside the dead. I see a father give something to his daughter, a packet of pills. "If they try to do anything to you . . . ," he says. Occasionally the train stops and a few people from each car are ordered to get out to fetch water. Magda takes the bucket once. "We're in Poland," she tells us when she returns. Later she explains how she knows. When she went for water, a man out in his field had yelled a greeting to her in Polish and in German, telling her the name of the town and gesturing frantically, drawing his finger across his neck. "Just trying to scare us," Magda says.

The train moves on and on. Magda cusses under her breath. Is it healthier to get the bad thoughts out, or swallow them? My parents slump on either side of me. They don't speak. I never see them touch. My father's beard is growing in gray. He looks older than his father, and it frightens me. I beg him to shave. I have no way of knowing that youthfulness could indeed save a life when we reach the end of this journey. It's just a gut feeling, just a girl missing the father she knows, longing for him to be the bon vivant again, the debonair flirt, the ladies' man. I don't want him to become like the father with the pills who mutters to his family, "This is worse than death."

But when I kiss my father's cheek and say, "Papa, please shave," he answers me with anger. "What for?" he says. "What for? What for?" I'm ashamed that I've said the wrong thing and made him annoyed with me. Why did I say the wrong thing? Why did I think it was my job to tell my father what to do? I remember his rage when I lost the tuition money for school. I lean against my mother for comfort. I wish my parents would reach for each other instead of sitting as strangers. My mother doesn't say much. But she doesn't moan either. She doesn't wish to be dead. She simply goes inside herself.

"Dicuka," she says into the dark one night, "listen. We don't know where we're going. We don't know what's going to happen. Just remember, no one can take away from you what you've put in your mind."

I fall into another dream of Eric. I wake again.

They open the cattle car doors, and the bright May sun slashes in. We are desperate to get out. We rush toward the air and the light. We practically fall out of the car, tumbling against one another in our hurry to descend. After several days of the ceaseless motion of the train, it's hard to stand upright on firm ground. In every way we are trying to get our bearings—piece out our location, steady our nerves and our limbs. I see the crowded dark of winter coats amassed on a narrow stretch of dirt. I see the flash of white in someone's scarf or cloth bundle of belongings, the yellow of the mandatory stars. I see the sign: ARBEIT MACHT FREI. Work sets you free. Music plays. My father is suddenly cheerful. "You see," he says, "it can't be a terrible place." He looks as though he would dance if the platform weren't so crowded. "We'll only work a little, till the war's over," he says. The rumors we heard at the brick factory must be true. We must be here to work. I search for the ripple of nearby fields and imagine Eric's lean body across from me, bending to tend a crop. Instead, I see unbroken horizontal lines: the boards on the cattle cars, the endless wire of a fence, low-slung buildings. In the distance, a few trees and chimneys break the flat plane of this barren place.

Men in uniform push among us. Nobody explains anything. They just bark simple directions. *Go here. Go there.* The Nazis point and shove. The men are herded into a separate line. I see my father wave to us. Maybe they're being sent ahead to stake out a place for their families. I wonder where we'll sleep tonight. I wonder when we'll eat. My mother, Magda, and I stand together in a long line of women and children. We inch forward. We approach the man who, with a conductor's wave of a finger, will deliver us to our fates. I do not yet know that this man is Dr. Josef Mengele, the infamous Angel of Death. As we advance toward him, I can't look away from his eyes, so domineering, so cold. When we've drawn nearer, I can see a boyish flash of gapped teeth when he grins. His voice is almost kind when he asks if anyone is sick and sends those who say yes to the left.

"If you're over fourteen and under forty, stay in this line," another officer says. "Over forty, move left." A long line of the elderly and children and mothers holding babies branches off to the left.

My mother links her arm with mine. "Button your coat," she says. "Stand tall."

She has gray hair, all gray, early gray, but her face is as smooth and unlined as mine. Magda and I squeeze our mother between us. My hair is tucked back under a scarf.

My mother scolds me again to stand tall. "You're a woman, not a child," she says. But I don't want to let go of her hand. The line is moving. Dr. Mengele is pointing. Now it's our turn.

"Is she your mother or your sister?" he asks, his finger lifted in the air, ready to signal our fate.

I cling to my mother's hand. Magda hugs her other side. My mother could pass for my sister. But I don't think about which word will protect her: "mother" or "sister." I don't think at all.

"Mother," I say.

Dr. Mengele points my mother to the left. I start to follow her. He grabs my shoulder. "You're going to see your mother very soon," he says. "She's just going to take a shower." He pushes Magda and me to the right.

We don't know the meaning of left versus right. "Where are we going now?" we ask each other. "What will happen to us?" We're marched to a different part of the sparse campus. Only women surround us, most young. Some look bright, almost giddy, glad to be breathing fresh air and enjoying the sun on their skin after the relentless stench and claustrophobic dark of the train. Others chew their lips. Fear circulates among us, but curiosity, too.

We're stopped in front of more low buildings. Women in striped dresses stand around us. We soon learn that they are the inmates charged with governing the others, but we don't know yet that we're prisoners here. I've unbuttoned my coat in the steady sun, and one of the girls in a striped dress eyes my blue silk. She walks toward me, cocking her head.

"Well, look at you," she says in Polish. She kicks dust on my low-heeled shoes. Before I realize what's happening, she reaches for the tiny coral earrings set in gold that, in keeping with Hungarian custom, have been in my ears since birth. She yanks, and I feel a sharp sting. She pockets the earrings.

In spite of the physical hurt, I feel desperate for her to like me. As ever, I want to belong. Her humiliating sneer hurts more than my ripped earlobes. "Why did you do that?" I say. "I would have given you the earrings."

"I was rotting here while you were free, going to school, going to the theater," she says.

I wonder how long she's been here. She's thin but sturdy. She stands tall. She could be a dancer. I wonder why she seems so angry that I have reminded her of normal life. "When will I see my mother?" I ask her. "I was told I'd see her soon."

She gives me a cold, sharp stare. There is no empathy in her eyes. There is nothing but rage. She points to the smoke rising up from one of the chimneys in the distance. "Your mother is burning in there," she says. "You better start talking about her in the past tense."

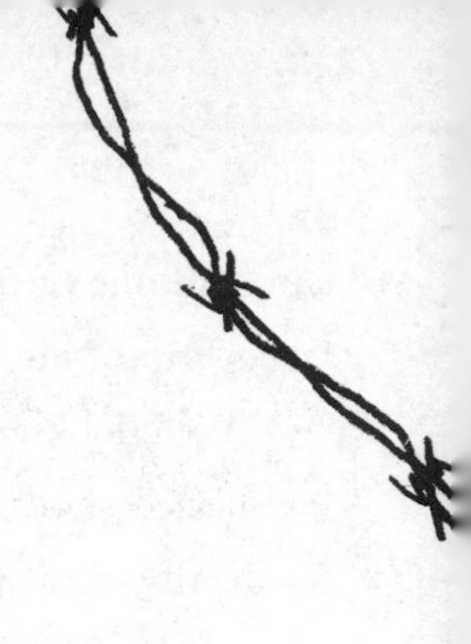

Chapter 6

DANCING IN HELL

Magda stares at the chimney on top of the building our mother entered. "The soul never dies," she says. My sister finds words of comfort. But I am in shock. I am numb. I can't think about the incomprehensible things that are happening, that have already happened. I can't picture my mother consumed by flames. I can't fully grasp that she is gone. And I can't ask why. I can't even grieve. Not now. It will take all of my attention to survive the next minute, the next breath. I will survive if my sister is there. I will survive by attaching myself to her as though I am her shadow.

We are herded through the silent yet echoing showers. We are robbed of our hair. We stand outside, shorn and naked, waiting for our uniforms. Taunts from the *kapos* and SS officers swarm us like arrows grazing our bare, wet skin. Worse than their words are their eyes. I'm sure the disgust with which they glare at us could tear my skin, split my ribs. Their hate is both possessive and dismissive, and it makes me ill. Once I thought that Eric would be the first man to see me naked. Now he will never see my flesh unscarred by their hatred. Have they already made me something less than human? Will I ever resemble the girl I was? *I will never forget your eyes, your hands*. I have to keep myself together, if not for myself then for Eric.

I turn to my sister, who has fallen into her own shocked silence, who has managed in each chaotic dash from place to place, in every crowded line, not to leave my side. She shivers as the sun falls. She holds in her hands her shorn locks, thick strands of her ruined hair. We have been standing naked for hours, and she grips her hair as though in holding it she can hold on to herself, her humanity. She is so near that we are almost touching, and yet I long for her. Magda. The confident, sexy girl with all the jokes. Where is she? She seems to be asking the same question. She searches for herself in her ragged clumps of hair.

The contradictions in this place unnerve me. Murder, we've just learned, is efficient here. Systematic. But there seems to be no system in place for distributing the uniforms for which we've been waiting most of the day. The guards are cruel and rigid, yet it seems that no one is in charge. The scrutiny they give our bodies doesn't signal our value; it signifies only the degree to which we have been forgotten by the world. Nothing makes sense. But this, too, the interminable waiting, the complete absence of reason, must be part of the design. How can I keep myself steady in a place where the only steadiness is in fences, in death, in humiliation, in the steadily churning smoke?

Magda finally speaks to me. "How do I look?" she asks. "Tell me the truth."

The truth? She looks like a mangy dog. A naked stranger. I can't tell her this, of course, but any lie would hurt too much, and so I must find an impossible answer, a truth that doesn't wound. I think of Maria in *For Whom the Bell Tolls*, the charming way she raked her fingers through her short curls. Six more months and it will grow back, she told Roberto. I gaze into the fierce blue of my sister's eyes and think that even for her to ask the question "How do I look?" is the bravest thing I've ever heard. There aren't mirrors here. She is asking me to help her find and face herself. And so I tell her the one true thing that's mine to say.

"Your eyes," I tell my sister, "they're so beautiful. I never noticed them when they were covered up by all that hair." It's the first time I see that we have a choice: to pay attention to what we've lost or to pay attention to what we still have.

"Thank you," she whispers.

The other things I want to ask her, tell her, seem better left wordless. Words can't give shape to this new reality. To the gray coat of my mama's shoulder as I lean on her and the train goes on and on. To my papa's face overgrown with shadow. To the impossibility of having those dark and hungry hours back again. To the transformation of my parents into smoke. Both of my parents. I must assume my father is dead too. I am about to muster a voice to ask Magda if we dare hope that we haven't been totally orphaned in the space of a day, but I see that Magda has let her hair fall out of her fingers and onto the dusty ground.

They bring the uniforms—gray, ill-fitting dresses made of scratchy cotton and wool. The sky is going dark. They herd us to the gloomy, primitive barracks, where we will sleep on tiered shelves, six to a board. It is a relief to go into the ugly room, to lose sight of the endlessly smoking chimney. The *kapo*, the young woman who stole my earrings, assigns us bunks and explains the rules. No one is allowed outside at night. There is the bucket—our nighttime bathroom. With our bunkmates, Magda and I try lying on our board on the top tier. We discover there's more room if we alternate heads and feet. Still, no one person can roll over or adjust her position without displacing someone else. We work out a system for rolling together, coordinating our turns. The *kapo* distributes a bowl to each new inmate. "Don't lose it," she warns. "If you don't have a bowl, you don't eat." In the darkening barracks, we stand waiting for the next command. I recognize some of the women and girls from Kassa, though they are unrecognizable. Girls who went to my Jewish elementary school. I remember their names. Lily. Marta. I even see one of my former teachers from that school. But we don't speak. We wait for instructions. We wonder. Will we be fed a meal? Will we be sent to sleep? We hear music. I think I must be imagining the sound of woodwinds and strings, but another inmate explains there is a camp orchestra here, led by a world-class violinist. *Klara!* I think. But the violinist she mentions is Viennese.

We hear clipped voices speaking German outside the barracks. The *kapo* pulls herself straight as the door rattles open. There on the threshold I recognize the uniformed officer from the selection line. I know it's him, the way he smiles with his lips parted, the gap between his front teeth. Dr. Mengele, we learn. He is a refined killer and a lover of the arts. He trawls among the barracks in the evenings, searching for talented inmates to entertain him. He walks in tonight with his entourage of assistants and casts his gaze like a net over the new arrivals with our baggy dresses and our hastily shorn hair. We stand still, backs to the wooden bunks that edge the room. He examines us. Magda ever so subtly grazes my hand with hers. Dr. Mengele barks out a question, and before I know what is happening, the girls standing nearest me, who know I trained as a ballerina and gymnast back in Kassa, push me forward, closer to the Angel of Death.

He studies me. I don't know where to put my eyes. I stare straight ahead at the open door. The orchestra is assembled just outside. They are silent, awaiting orders. I feel like Salome, made to dance for her stepfather, Herod, lifting veil after veil to expose her flesh. Does the dance give her power, or does the dance strip it away?

"Little dancer," Dr. Mengele says, "dance for me." He directs the musicians to begin playing. The familiar opening strain of "The Blue Danube" waltz filters into the dark, close room. Mengele's eyes bulge at me. I'm lucky. I know a routine to "The Blue Danube" that I can dance in my sleep. But my limbs are heavy, as in a nightmare when there's danger and you can't run away. "Dance!" he commands again, and I feel my body start to move.

First the high kick. Then the pirouette and turn. The splits.

And up. As I step and bend and twirl, I can hear Mengele talking to his assistant. He never takes his eyes off me, but he attends to his duties as he watches. I can hear his voice over the music. He discusses with the other officer which ones of the hundred girls present will be killed next. If I miss a step, if I do anything to displease him, it could be me. I dance. I dance. I am dancing in hell. I can't bear to see the executioner as he decides our fates. I close my eyes.

I hear my ballet master's voice from that far-off world before barracks and chimneys and Mengele. "All your ecstasy in life is going to come from the inside," my ballet master said. I never understood what he meant. But now those words come back. I focus on my routine, on my years of training—each line and curve of my body like a syllable in verse, my body telling a story: A girl arrives at a dance. She spins in excitement and anticipation. Then she pauses to reflect and observe. What will happen in the hours ahead? Whom will she meet? She turns toward a fountain, arms sweeping up and around to embrace the scene. She bends to pick up flowers and tosses them one at a time to her admirers and fellow revelers, throwing flowers to the people, handing out tokens of love. I can hear the violins swell. My heart races. In the private darkness within, I hear my mother's words come back to me, as though she is there in the barren room, whispering below the music. *Just remember, no one can take away from you what you've put in your own mind.* Dr. Mengele, my fellow starved-to-the-bone inmates, the defiant who will survive, and the soon-to-be-dead, even my beloved sister disappear, and the only world that exists is the one inside my head. "The Blue Danube" fades, and now I can hear Tchaikovsky's "Romeo and Juliet." The barracks floor becomes a stage at the Budapest opera house. I dance for my fans in the audience. I dance within the glow of hot lights. I dance for my lover, Romeo, as he lifts me high above the stage. I dance for love. I dance for life.

As I dance, a shocking thought bolts through me. I can see that Dr. Mengele, the seasoned killer who just this morning murdered my mother, is more pitiful than me. I am free in my mind, which he can never be. He will always have to live with what he's done. He is more a prisoner than I am. As I close my routine with a final, graceful split, I pray, but it isn't myself I pray for. I pray for him. I pray, for his sake, that he won't have the need to kill me.

He must be impressed by my performance, because he tosses me a loaf of bread—a gesture, as it turns out, that will later save my life. As evening turns to night, I share the bread with Magda and our bunkmates. I am grateful to have bread. I am grateful to be alive.

In my first weeks at Auschwitz, I learn the rules of survival. If you can steal a piece of bread from the guards, you are a hero, but if you steal from an inmate, you are disgraced, and you die; competition and domination get you nowhere. Cooperation is the name of the game; to survive is to transcend your own needs and commit yourself to someone or something outside yourself. For me, that someone is Magda. That something is the hope that I will see Eric again tomorrow, when I am free.

We wake at 4:00 a.m. for the *Appell*, the roll call, and stand in the freezing dark to be counted and recounted before we're assigned to our work posts for the day. The guards say that if you're not feeling well, you can stay behind and they will take you to the hospital, but we learn there is no hospital. If you stay behind, you're never seen again. If you don't feel well, pretend that you're fine. Ignore the cold, the hunger, the hurt, all that makes you unwell. Stand and be counted. March to work.

Often when we walk to work, I can see the Angel of Death conducting the selection line, welcoming new arrivals. I hate him. He killed my mother. His finger issues death. His existence fills me with paralyzing fear. And yet he saved my life. Twice already, he's let me live. The person who delivered my biggest loss, who casts us with a daily, ever-present fear, is also the person responsible for my life. How strange to feel gratitude alongside my rage and dread.

Most days I'm assigned to work in a warehouse called Canada, where we're made to sort the belongings of the newly arrived inmates. Sometimes Magda works there with me, opening dusty luggage, touching the material of so many hundreds and thousands of strangers' lives. Clothes, photographs, cherished heirlooms, the practical and the sacred jumbled together in piles. I wonder where our suitcase is, the one my mother hastily packed for the brick factory. I wonder if I would recognize it now, or if the objects inside would appear to me like remnants of strangers' lives. In a way, those people we were mere weeks ago have become strangers. They wouldn't in a million years recognize us now, our faces thinned from scant food and constant fear. Is my father still alive? I can't ask Magda. I can't form it in words, this unanswerable question.

As horrible and strange as it is to sort through the leftovers of lives cut short, working in Canada is a coveted job. We get to be indoors. We're allowed to drink water throughout the day. Some of the guards are even kind, speaking to us as though we're human beings, not a filthy scourge. Sometimes we find food tucked away in the luggage—hard cheese, old bread. Stale food is of no use to Germany, so the guards turn their heads while we harvest the crumbs of meals from people who might already be dead.

There are worse jobs at Auschwitz. Some days we work at the crematoria, removing gold teeth, hair, and skin from the corpses waiting to be burned. The first time we're forced to pull teeth from dead bodies, Lily vomits. I rub her back. I wipe her face with the hem of my dress. "Go someplace else in your mind," I tell her. "Don't let it infect you."

This is how we survive; this is how we dance in hell: we use the gift of our minds. When we're sad, we sing French love songs. When we're starving, we feast. We cook in our heads. We prepare elaborate feasts, fighting over how much paprika you put in Hungarian chicken paprikash, or how to make the best seven-layer chocolate cake. As we clean and clean and clean the barracks, as we march, as we scavenge off luggage and corpses, we talk as though we're heading to market, planning our weekly menu, testing each fruit and vegetable for ripeness. We give one another cooking lessons. Here's how to make *palacsinta*, Hungarian crepes. How thin the pancake must be. How much sugar to use. How many nuts. Do you put caraway in your *székely gulyás*? Do you use two onions? No, three. No, just one and a half. We salivate over our imaginary dishes, and as we eat our one actual meal of the day—watery soup, a stale piece of bread—I talk about the goose my mother kept in the attic and fed with corn each day, its liver bulging, more and more, until it was time to slaughter the goose and blend its liver into pâté. And when we fall onto our bunks at night and finally sleep, we dream of food then too. The village clock chimes 10:00 a.m., and my father slips into our apartment with a package from the butcher across the street. Today, a cut of pork hidden in newspaper. "Dicuka, come taste," he beckons. "What a role model you are," my mother gripes, "feeding a Jewish girl pork." But she is almost smiling. She's making strudel, stretching the phyllo dough over the dining room table, working it with her hands and blowing underneath it until it's paper thin.

The tang of peppers and cherries in my mother's strudel; her deviled eggs; the pasta she cut by hand, so fast I feared she'd lose a finger; especially the challah, our Friday-night bread. For my mother, food was as much about the artistry of creating it as it was about enjoying the finished meal. We are artists, too, in the barracks, always in the thick of creating. What we make in our minds provides its own kind of sustenance.

Our imaginations thrive; our bodies dwindle. We stop getting our periods. Marta thinks it's from poor nutrition. Magda thinks we're being drugged. I think of the streaks of red on my white skirt, the startle of my mother's slap. How minor those surprises seem now. I can't tell if the pain is worse when I think of my mother, or when I don't. I think of Eric instead. Sunlight brightening his hair, his hands on my waist.

One night I wake with abdominal cramps and the burning need to empty my bowels. We aren't allowed to leave the barracks at night. But I am ashamed to squat over the bucket in the dark. I am afraid it will overflow. I don't want Magda to see me, to worry that I'm sick. I rush outside to the latrine. I barely make it in time. I cry with relief. I cry with pain. I used to be strong. I used to do the splits and climb a rope to the ceiling. Will I ever be that person again? Or will my body keep betraying me with proof that I am changed, that I am weak, that I am less than I used to be?

I walk back to the barracks by moonlight. A harsh voice cuts through the quiet.

"Halt!" It's the Polish *kapo*, the girl who ripped out my earrings the day we arrived. "You've broken the rules," she says. "You will be punished."

She makes me stand against the outside of the barracks, my hands pressed against the cold wall. She swings at my back with some kind of belt or rope. It looks like a dog leash. The humiliation hurts worse than the sting of the whip. I'm nothing to her. I am worse than no one.

Magda wakes up as I climb back onto the bunk, my back on fire.

"Where were you, Dicu?" she asks, worry in her voice.

"Nowhere," I say. It feels like truth. It feels like escape. I am no one. I am nowhere.

I never tell Magda what happened with the *kapo*, but I sense her watching me more carefully in the days that follow. When we're assigned to different workstations, she is greedy with me at the evening meal, wanting my words, my attention. If I disappear, she won't make it. I force myself to be cheerful, to put aside a portion of the hard bread served each night to share with her in the morning.

A few nights after the beating, we enact a beauty pageant in the barracks before bed. It's Esther's idea. She's a married woman, a little older than Magda, who sleeps in the bunk next to ours. Lily and Marta join in, and Zsuzsi, the wealthy girl whose family owned the cherry orchards where my mother would take us to pick fruit in the summer. We model in our gray, shapeless dresses, our dingy underwear. There's a Hungarian saying that beauty is all in the shoulders. Nobody can strike a pose like Magda. She wins the pageant. But no one is ready for sleep.

"Here's a better competition," Magda says. "Who's got the best boobs?"

We strip in the dark and parade around with our chests sticking out. Mere months ago I was working out for more than five hours a day in the studio. I would ask my father to beat my stomach to feel how strong I was. I could even pick him up and carry him. Now I stand topless and freezing in the barracks. I force myself to strut around in the dark like a model. Lily and Marta follow my lead. We sway our hips; we get lost in the show, this charade of loving our bodies.

But when the girls decide that I have won the contest, I feel a flush of real pride. For a moment, I feel beautiful. Valuable.

"My famous sister," Magda says as we drift off to sleep.

Chapter 7
BLUE BODIES

Time feels shapeless in a death camp. Days: innumerable and indistinct. Outlook: bleak. The hours roll on and on, yet nothing changes. *Appell.* Work. Soup. Smoke. Weeks and months pass, and the weather cools. We're issued old coats. The guards just toss us the coats, willy-nilly, with no attention to size. It is up to us to find the one with the best fit and fight for it. Magda is lucky. They throw her a thick warm coat, long and heavy, with buttons all the way up to the neck. It is so warm, so coveted. But she trades it instantly. The coat she chooses in its place is a flimsy little thing, barely to the knees, showing off plenty of chest. Anger flares in me. What is she thinking? Doesn't she want to survive? Am I not worth surviving for? Yet as I watch Magda strut and preen in her new coat, I realize that for her, wearing something sexy is a better survival tool than staying warm. Feeling attractive gives her something inside, a sense of dignity, more valuable to her than physical comfort.

I watch my fellow inmates. I see how many of the girls are like Magda, managing to conjure an inner world, a haven, even when their eyes are open. One girl in our barracks somehow saved a picture of herself from before internment, a picture in which she still had long hair. I don't know where she keeps the picture, but I see her holding it sometimes, gazing at herself, as though this artifact from her life before can remind her who she really is, assure her that that person still exists.

Another girl finds a shard of a mirror in the latrine. Perhaps someone pilfered it from Canada and left it where others could use it. This girl holds the piece of mirror up to her face, speaks to herself in the glass, tilting her head, transforming herself, transporting herself. She's Marie Antoinette, arriving at the French court, stepping into her destiny as the next and final queen of France. It's playacting. And it's hope.

I realize I can fantasize, too, that I can dream without limit. The collective fantasies—the meals, the feasts, the banquets—are sustaining. The private ones are too. Always my fantasies are of Eric. I sit in an outdoor café in Košice after the war. My hair is long. I'm wearing a green silk dress and slippers with heels and ankle straps, sipping coffee, reading a book of philosophy, lost in deep thought.

"Editke," a voice says, lifting me out of abstract ideas and into the warm sun, the bright world.

I feel it in my body even before I confirm it with sight. A stirring that calls me to rise from my chair, to step toward the man who has spoken my name with such tenderness and regard. With such love.

I'm in his arms. He lifts me off the ground. I bury my face in his neck. He sets me down so he can cup my face in his hands.

"We made it," he says. His green eyes brim with happy tears.

Then a kiss. So warm, so loving and passionate, his hands pressing at the small of my back, my body melting in his arms.

We laugh when we realize that I'm still holding my book, a finger tucked inside to mark my place. He takes the book, closes it.

"Come home with me," he says. Nothing can stop us from being together now. I clasp his hand as we walk along the park that runs through the center of the main avenue. I hear birdsong and children playing. My fantasy brings us to his doorstep, up the stairs to his bright, airy apartment, onto the sofa in the parlor, where he pulls me onto his lap. My fantasy even brings us into his bedroom.

But then I run short. What happens in a bedroom? Kissing and undressing, but what else? There are so many things I can do with my body, but the postures and choreography of love are beyond imagining. I need information.

Esther, the young woman who sleeps in the bunk next to mine, was married before the war. I pump her for details. But my vocabulary is meager.

"What is it like?" I ask her one night. "To belong to a man?"

"Do you mean marriage," she asks, "or sex?"

I know Magda and the other girls must be listening. "Marriage," I say. But I mean both.

Someone titters in the dark.

"Sex," someone else says. "Tell us about the sex."

"Well," Esther says, her voice lowering to a throaty whisper, "a man's body is different from ours. He has something, a part that hangs between his legs. When he's filled with desire, it stiffens. He puts it inside you."

"Mmm," another girl fake moans.

I feel irritated. This isn't a joke to me. It's a matter of having the details I need to stoke hope, to dream of a future where fear and starvation end and love lives.

"The place he puts it—this is the place that opens for a baby to come out?"

"Yes," she says.

The whole barracks rings with laughter. I am undeterred.

"And it feels good?" I ask.

"Oh yes," she says. "It feels . . ." She drops off, perhaps searching for the right word, or perhaps lost in her own fantasy.

I hold my breath, waiting for her to continue.

"There's no better feeling," she finally says. "And then it's so good to fall asleep on his chest."

In her sigh, I hear the echo of something beautiful, unharmed by loss. I see marriage not as my parents lived it but as something luminous. I sense passion and pleasure and daily belonging. Love, whole love.

In my mind, I can have all of it.

I do my best to bend my mind toward hope, but real life intrudes. We are sent to the showers every day at Auschwitz, and every shower is fraught with uncertainty. We never know whether water or gas will stream out of the tap. One day when I feel the water falling down on us, I let out my breath. I spread greasy soap over my body. I'm not skin and bones yet. Here in the quiet after the fear, I can recognize myself. My arms and thighs and stomach are still taut with my dancer muscles. I slip into a fantasy of Eric. We are university students now, living in Budapest. We take our books to study at a café. His eyes leave the page and travel over my face. I feel him pausing over my eyes and lips. Just as I imagine lifting my face to receive his kiss, I realize how quiet the shower room has become. I feel a chill in my gut. The man I fear above all others stands at the door. The Angel of Death is gazing right at me. I stare at the floor, waiting for the others to begin breathing again so that I know he is gone. But he doesn't leave.

"You!" he calls. "My little dancer."

I try to hear Eric's voice more loudly than Mengele's. *I'll never forget your eyes. I'll never forget your hands.*

"Come," he orders.

I follow. What else can I do? I walk toward the buttons on his coat, avoiding the eyes of my fellow inmates, because I can't stand the thought of seeing my fear mirrored there. *Breathe, breathe*, I tell myself. He leads me, naked and wet, down a hall and into an office with a desk and a chair. Water runs from my body onto the cold floor. He leans against the desk and looks me over, taking his time. I am too terrified to think, but little currents of impulse move through my body like reflexes. Kick him. A high kick to the face. Drop to the floor in a little ball and hold myself tight. I hope that whatever he plans to do to me will be over quickly.

"Come closer," he says.

I face him as I inch forward, but I don't see him. I focus only on the living part of me, the *yes I can, yes I can.* I feel his body as I near him. A menthol smell. The taste of tin can on my tongue. As long as I'm shaking, I know I'm alive. His fingers work over his buttons. *Yes I can, yes I can.* I think of my mama and her long, long hair. The way she'd wind it up on top of her head and let it down like a curtain at night. I'm naked with her murderer, but he can't ever take her away. Just as I am close enough for him to touch me, with fingers that I determine not to feel, a phone rings in another room. He flinches. He rebuttons his coat.

"Don't move," he orders as he opens the door.

I hear him pick up the phone in the next room, his voice neutral and curt. I don't make a decision. I run. The next thing I know I'm sitting beside my sister as we devour the daily ladle of soup, the little pieces of potato skin in the weak broth bobbing up at us like scabs. The fear that he will find me again and punish me, that he will finish what he started, that he will select me for death never leaves me. It never goes away. I don't know what will happen next. But in the meantime I can keep myself alive inside. *I survived today*, I chant in my head. *I survived today. Tomorrow I will be free.*

We can choose what the horror teaches us. We make up our own minds about how much suffering we can endure. There are many ways to die at Auschwitz. Gunshot. Starvation. Disease. Gas. Torture. These are the ways the Nazis choose. But prisoners also choose when they have had enough, when they are done with a life that isn't life. They stop eating, refuse to get out of bed in the morning, hang themselves, ingest poison, throw themselves on the electrified fences. Sometimes when we wake up in the morning or when we walk back to the barracks from work, we see bodies, dozens of bodies, burning on the fence. The guards shut off the electricity and force inmates to pull the charred bodies off the wire. I try to think of them as people who died in flight. Who took the only freedom they could claim. Yet they terrify me, these corpses gone blue. This is the end of the line, where hopelessness leads. It's an ugly death, an anguish. I watch Magda and the girls around me for signs of despair.

Zsuzsi, the wealthy girl from home, begins to withdraw. It happens slowly, over days or more. She speaks less, and her eyes look dull. She's slow to cooperate with camp routines. I have to drag her with me, consumed by the feeling that I can't leave her behind. As we walk to Canada, I try to cheer her up, I mention the cherry-picking and the tart-sweet cherry jam. I try to think of something funny to say. She looks at me flatly.

One evening at dinner I notice that she doesn't touch her soup.

"Let her be," Magda says.

"Why, so you can eat her soup?" I retort. My anger surprises me.

I know I've gone too far and hurt my sister when she replies, "Maybe you're too young, too much the baby of the family, to know when you're being a pest, to know when you're not needed."

I can't sleep that night. I struggle to imagine anything beyond my hunger and pain and dread. The next morning, I drag myself into line for *Appell*, my feet heavy, head thick. Just as I remember that I haven't looked for Zsuzsi, a dark shape darts toward the fence. It's Zsuzsi. If I run to her, I'll be shot. If I yell to her, she will be shot. Either path leads to death.

"Look away," Magda whispers.

But I can't. My eyes are fixed on Zsuzsi as she hits the fence. It's my fault. I was too caught up in my own hurt to check in with her when we woke up. There's something I could have done or said, I know it, some difference I could have made.

"Dicu," Magda says that night in bed, "she already decided what she was going to do."

"I was selfish," I say. "I wasn't thinking of her or anyone else."

"If you think you could have changed her mind, then you must think you're God," Magda replies.

I try to resist the truth of her words, I start to build my case, that I am to blame or that God is, but my sister squeezes my hand.

"Sleep, Dicuka," she says.

I close my eyes. I will my breath to fill my belly, my chest. I push it out. I follow the rhythm, feeling sleepiness take hold.

"If you're okay," Magda says, her voice a soft whisper, "then I'm okay."

I feel her warmth beside me, I think of Eric. *Tomorrow*, I tell myself. Not someday. Not maybe. *Tomorrow*. Hope is a rising in my chest, a feeling when I swallow, a sweetness in the throat.

Chapter 8

A CARTWHEEL

True winter comes, snow and bitter cold, our coats no match for the slicing wind. Anna, a girl in my barracks, develops a cough. She tosses in her bunk at night, retching and choking. Every morning I expect to find her dead on her bunk, and I fear at every selection line that her cough will betray, that she'll be sent toward death. But she surprises me. She manages to gather strength each morning to work another day and keeps a lively spark in her eyes each time she faces Mengele's pointing finger in a selection line. At night she collapses back onto her bunk, breathing in rasps.

"How do you keep going?" I ask her one night. Is there a prayer she says, an image she holds in her mind, something I can remind her of if she gets worse, something I can save for a time when Magda or I might hit despair?

"I heard we're going to be liberated by Christmas," she says.

She keeps a meticulous calendar in her head, counting down the days and hours until our liberation, determined to live to be free.

Part of me wants to gird her against disappointment. What does she know about the workings of war? She holds no map of the Allied fronts. She's built a certainty out of a rumor. Yet I realize that Christmas is her Eric, her countdown as restorative and necessary as my imagined reunion.

"Tomorrow," she says on Christmas Eve.

"Tomorrow," I say back.

All Christmas Day she pauses to listen, to lift her eyes to the farthest line of fence, breath fogging the air around her head, a smile on her chapped lips. But our liberators don't come. The next morning, Anna is dead.

One morning shortly after Christmas, we stand in yet another line. The cold bites. We are to be tattooed. I wait my turn. I roll up my sleeve. I present my arm. I am responding automatically, making the motions required of me, so cold and hungry, so cold and hungry that I am almost numb. *Does anyone know I'm here?* I used to wonder that all the time, and now the question comes at me sluggishly, as if through a dense and constant fog. I can't remember how I used to think. I have to remind myself to picture Eric, but if I think about him too consciously, I can't re-create his face. I have to trick myself into memory, catch myself unawares. *Where's Magda?* That's the first thing I ask when I wake, when we march to work, before we crash into sleep. I dart my eyes around to confirm that she's still behind me. Even if our eyes don't meet, I know that she is also keeping watch for me.

The officer with the needle and ink is right in front of me now. He grabs my wrist and starts to prick, but then shoves me aside. "I'm not going to waste the ink on you," he says. He pushes me into a different line.

"This line is death," the girl nearest me says. "This is the end." She is completely gray, as though she's covered in dust. Someone ahead of us in the line is praying. In a place where the threat of death is constant, this moment still pierces me. I think suddenly about the difference between deadly and deadening. Auschwitz is both. The chimneys smoke and smoke. Any moment could be the last one. So why care? Why invest? And yet, if this moment, this very one, is my last on Earth, do I have to waste it in resignation and defeat? Must I spend it as if I'm already dead?

"We never know what the lines mean," I tell the girl nearest me. What if the unknown could make us curious instead of gutting us with fear? And then I see Magda. She's been selected for a different line. If I'm sent to die, if I'm sent to work, if they evacuate me to a different camp as they've begun to do to others . . . Nothing matters except that I stay with my sister, that she stay with me. We are of the few, the lucky inmates who have not yet been completely cut off from our families. It is no exaggeration to say that I live for my sister. It is no exaggeration to say that my sister lives for me. There is chaos in the yard. I don't know what the lines mean. The only thing I know is that I must pass to whatever lies ahead *with Magda.* Even if what lies ahead is death. I eye the gap of crusted-over snow that separates us. Guards ring us. I don't have a plan. Time is slow and time is fast. Magda and I share a glance. I see her blue eyes. And then I am in motion. I am doing cartwheels, hands to earth, feet to sky, around, around. A guard stares at me. He's right side up. He's upside down. I expect a bullet any second. And I don't want to die, but I can't keep myself from turning around again and again. He doesn't raise his gun. Is he too surprised to shoot me? Am I too dizzy to see? He winks at me. I swear I see him wink. *Okay*, he seems to say, *this time you win.*

In the few seconds that I hold his complete attention, Magda runs across the yard into my line to join me. We melt back into the crowd of girls waiting for whatever will happen next.

We're herded across the icy yard toward the train platform where we arrived six months before, where we parted from our father, where we walked with our mother between us in the final moments of her life. Music played then; it's silent now. If wind is silence. The constant rush of burdensome cold, the wide-open sighing mouth of death and winter no longer sound like noise to me. My head teems with questions and dread, but these thoughts are so enduring, they don't feel like thoughts anymore. It is always almost the end.

We're just going to a place to work until the end of the war, we have been told. If we could hear even two minutes of news, we would know that the war itself might be the next casualty. As we stand there waiting to climb the narrow ramp into the cattle car, we have no way of knowing that the Russians are approaching Poland from one side and the Americans from the other. The Nazis are evacuating

Auschwitz bit by bit. The inmates we are leaving behind, those who can survive one more month at Auschwitz, will soon be free. We sit in the dark, waiting for the train to pull away. A soldier—part of the Wehrmacht, the German army, not the Nazi Party's SS forces—puts his head in the door and speaks to us in Hungarian. "You have to eat," he says. "No matter what they do, remember to eat, because you might get free, maybe soon." Is this hope he's offering us? Or false promise? A lie? This soldier is like the *nyilas* at the brick factory, spreading rumors, a voice of authority to silence our inner knowing. Who reminds a starving person to eat?

But even in the dark of the cattle car, his face backlit by miles of fence, miles of snow, I can tell that his eyes are kind. How strange that kindness now seems like a trick of the light.

I lose track of the time we are in motion. I sleep on Magda's shoulder, she on mine. Once I wake to my sister's voice. She is talking to someone I can't make out in the dark. "My teacher," she explains. The one from the brick factory, the one whose baby had cried and cried. At Auschwitz, all the women with small children were gassed from the start. The fact that she is still alive can mean only one thing: her baby died. Which is worse, I wonder, to be a child who has lost her mother or a mother who has lost her child? When the door opens, we're in Germany.

There are no more than a hundred of us. We're housed in what must be a children's summer camp, with bunk beds and a kitchen where, with scant provisions, we prepare our own meals.

In the morning, we are sent to work in a thread factory. We

wear leather gloves. We stop the spinning machine wheels to keep the threads from running together. Even with the gloves on, the wheels slice our hands. Magda's former teacher sits at a wheel next to Magda. She is crying loudly. I think it's because her hands are bleeding and sore. But she is weeping for Magda. "You need your hands," she moans. "You play piano. What will you do without your hands?"

The German forewoman who oversees our work silences her. "You're lucky to be working now," she says. "Soon you will be killed."

In the kitchen that night, we prepare our evening meal supervised by guards. "We've escaped the gas chamber," Magda says, "but we'll die making thread." It's funny because we *are* alive. We might not survive the war, but we have survived Auschwitz. I peel potatoes for our supper. Too accustomed to starvation rations, I am unable to waste any scrap of food. I hide the potato skins in my underwear. When the guards are in another room, I toast the peels in the oven. When we lift them eagerly to our mouths with our aching hands, the skins are still too hot to eat.

"We've escaped the gas chamber, but we'll die eating potato peels," someone says, and we laugh from a deep place in us that we didn't know still existed. We laugh, as I did every week at Auschwitz when we were forced to donate our blood for transfusions for wounded German soldiers. I would sit with the needle in my arm and humor myself. *Good luck winning a war with my pacifist dancer's blood!* I'd think. I couldn't yank my arm away, or I'd have been shot. I couldn't defy my oppressors with a gun or a fist. But I could find a way to my own power. And there's power in our laughter now. Our camaraderie, our lightheartedness reminds me of the night at Auschwitz when I won the boob contest. Our talk is sustenance.

"Who's from the best country?" a girl named Hava asks. We debate, singing the praises of home. "Nowhere is as beautiful as Yugoslavia," Hava insists. But this is an unwinnable competition. Home isn't a place anymore, not a country. It's a feeling, as universal as it is specific. If we talk too much about it, we risk it vanishing.

After a few weeks at the thread factory, the SS come for us one morning with striped dresses to replace our gray ones. We board yet another train. But this time we are forced on top of the cars in our striped uniforms, human decoys to discourage the British from bombing the train. It carries ammunition.

"From thread to bullets," someone says.

"Ladies, we've been handed a promotion," Magda says.

The wind on top of the boxcar is punishing, obliterating. But at least I can't feel hunger when I'm this cold. Would I rather die by cold or by fire? Gas or gun? It happens all of a sudden. Even with human prisoners on top of the trains, the British send the hiss and crash of bombs at us. Smoke. Shouts. The train stops, and I jump. I'm the first one down. I run straight up the snowy hillside that hugs the tracks toward a stand of thin trees, where I stop to scan the snow for my sister, catch my breath. Magda isn't there among the trees. I don't see her running from the train. Bombs hiss and erupt on the tracks. I can see a heap of bodies by the side of the train. Magda.

I have to choose. I can run. Escape into the forest. Scavenge a life. Freedom is that close, a matter of footsteps. But if Magda's alive and I abandon her, who will give her bread? And if she's dead? It's a second like a shutter's flap. *Click*: forest. *Click*: tracks. I run back down the hill.

Magda sits in the ditch, a dead girl in her lap. It's Hava. Blood streams from Magda's chin. In a nearby train car, men are eating. They're prisoners, too, but not like us. They're dressed in civilian clothes, not in uniforms. And they have food. German political prisoners, we guess. In any case, they are more privileged than we are. They're eating. Hava is dead and my sister lives and all I can think of is food. Magda, the beautiful one, is bleeding.

"Now that there's a chance to ask for some food, you look like this," I scold her. "You're too cut up to flirt." As long as I can be angry with her, I am spared from feeling fear, or the inverted, inside-out pain of what almost was. Instead of rejoicing, giving thanks that we are both alive, that we have survived another fatal moment, I am furious at my sister. I am furious at God, at fate, but I direct my confusion and hurt onto my sister's bleeding face.

Magda doesn't respond to my insult. She doesn't wipe away the blood. The guards circle in, shouting at us, prodding bodies with their guns to make sure that those who aren't moving are really dead. We leave Hava in the dirty snow and stand with the other survivors.

"You could have run," Magda says. She says it like I'm an idiot.

Within an hour, the ammunition has been reloaded into new

train cars and we're on top again in our striped uniforms, the blood dried on Magda's chin.

We are prisoners and refugees. We have long since lost track of the date, of time. Magda is my guiding star. As long as she is near, I have everything I need. We are pulled from the ammunition trains one morning, and we march many days in a row. The snow begins to melt, giving way to dead grass. Maybe we march for weeks. Bombs fall, sometimes close by. We can see cities burning. We stop in small towns throughout Germany, moving south sometimes, moving east, forced to work in factories along the way.

Counting inmates is the SS preoccupation. I don't count how many of us remain. Maybe I don't count because I know that each day the number is smaller. It's not a death camp. But there are dozens of ways to die. The roadside ditches run red with blood from those shot in the back or the chest—those who tried to run, those who couldn't keep up. Some girls' legs freeze, completely freeze, and they keel over like felled trees. Exhaustion. Exposure. Fever. Hunger. If the guards don't pull a trigger, the body does.

For days we have gone without food. We come to the crest of a hill and see a farm, outbuildings, a pen for livestock.

"One minute," Magda says. She runs toward the farm, weaving between trees, hoping not to be spotted by the SS who have stopped to smoke.

I watch Magda zigzag toward the garden fence. It's too early for spring vegetables, but I would eat cow feed. I would eat dried-up stalks. If a rat scurries near us in the dark where we sleep, girls pounce on it. I try not to call attention to Magda with my gaze. I look away, and when I glance back I can't see her. A gun fires. And again. Someone has spotted my sister. The guards yell at us, count us, guns drawn. A few more shots crack. There's no sight of Magda. *Help me. Help me.* I realize that I'm praying to my mother. I'm talking to her the way she used to pray to her mother's portrait over the piano. Even in labor she did this, Magda has told me. The night I was born, Magda heard our mother screaming, "Mother, help me!" Then Magda heard the baby cry—me—and our mother said, "You helped me." Calling on the dead is my birthright. *Mother, help us*, I pray. I see a flash of gray between the trees. Magda's alive. She escaped the bullets. And somehow, now, she escapes detection. I don't breathe until Magda stands with me again.

"There were potatoes," she says. "If those bastards hadn't started shooting, we'd be eating potatoes."

I imagine biting into one like an apple. I wouldn't even take the time to rub it clean. I would eat the dirt along with the starch, the skin.

We go to work in an ammunition factory near the Czech border. It is March, we learn. One morning I can't get off the bench in the shed-like dorms where we sleep. I'm burning with fever, shaking and weak.

"Get up, Dicuka," Magda orders me. "You can't call in sick." At Auschwitz, the ones who couldn't work were told they'd be taken to a hospital, but then they disappeared. Why would it be any different now? There's no infrastructure for killing here, no pipes laid, bricks mortared for the purpose. But a single bullet makes you just as dead. Still, I can't get up. I hear my own voice rambling about our grandparents. They'll let us skip school and take us to the bakery. Our mother can't take away the sweets. Somewhere in my head I know I am delirious, but I can't regain my senses. Magda tells me to shut up and covers me with a coat—to keep me warm if the fever breaks, she says, but more so to keep me hidden. "Don't move even a finger," she says.

The factory is nearby, across a little bridge over a fast stream. I lie under the coat, pretending not to exist, anticipating the moment I will be discovered missing and a guard will come into the shed to shoot me. Will Magda be able to hear the gunshot over the noise of the machines? I am no use to anyone now.

I swirl into delirious sleep. I dream of fire. It's a familiar dream—I have dreamed for nearly a year of being warm. Yet I wake from the dream, and this time the smell of smoke chokes me. Is the shed on fire? I am afraid to go to the door, afraid I won't make it on my weak legs, afraid that if I do, I'll give myself away. Then I hear the bombs. The whistle and blast. How did I sleep through the beginning of the attack? I pull myself off the bench. Where is the safest place? Even if I could run, where would I go? I hear shouts. "Factory's on fire! Factory's on fire!" someone yells.

I am aware again of the space between me and my sister: I have become an expert at measuring the space. How many hands between us? How many legs? Cartwheels? Now there's a bridge. Water and wood. And fire. I see it from the shed door where I finally stand and lean against the frame. The bridge to the factory is ablaze, the factory swallowed in smoke. For anyone who has lived through the bombing, the chaos is a respite. An opportunity to run. I picture Magda pushing out a window and dashing for the trees. Looking up through the branches toward the sky. Ready to run even as far as that to be free. If she makes a run for it, then I'm off the hook. I can slide back down to the floor and never get up. What a relief it will be. To exist is such an obligation. I let my legs fold up like scarves. I relax into the fall. And there is Magda in a halo of flame. Already dead. Beating me to it. I'll catch up. I feel the heat from the fire. Now I'll join her. Now. "I'm coming!" I call. "Wait for me!"

I don't catch the moment when she stops being a phantom and becomes flesh again. Somehow she makes me understand: She has crossed the burning bridge to return to me.

"You idiot," I say. "You could have run."

It's April now. Grass bursts green on the hills. Light stretches each day. Children spit at us as we pass through the outskirts of a town. How sad, I think, that these children have been brainwashed to hate me.

"You know how I'm going to get revenge?" Magda says. "I'm going to kill a German mother. A German kills my mother; I'm going to kill a German mother."

I have a different wish. I wish for the boy who spits at us to one day see that he doesn't have to hate. In my revenge fantasy, the boy who yells at us now—"Dirty Jew! Vermin!"—holds out a bouquet of roses. "Now I know," he says, "there's no reason to hate you. No reason at all." We embrace in mutual absolution. I don't tell Magda my fantasy.

One day as dusk comes, the SS shove us into a community hall where we'll sleep for the night. There's no food again.

"Anyone who leaves the premises will be shot immediately," the guard warns.

"Dicuka," Magda moans as we sink onto the wooden boards that will be our bed, "soon it's going to be the end for me."

"Shut up," I say. She is scaring me. Her despondence is more terrifying to me than a raised gun. She doesn't talk like this. She doesn't give up. Maybe I've been a burden to her. Maybe keeping me strong through my illness has depleted her. "You're not going to die," I tell her. "We're going to eat tonight."

"Oh, Dicuka," she says, and rolls toward the wall.

I'll show her. I'll show her there's hope. I'll get a little food. I'll revive her. The SS have gathered near the door, near the last evening light, to eat their rations. Sometimes they'll throw a scrap of food at us just for the pleasure of seeing us grovel. I go to them on my knees. "Please, please," I beg. They laugh. One soldier holds a wedge of canned meat toward me and I lunge for it, but he puts it in his mouth and they all laugh harder. They play with me like this until I am worn out. Magda is asleep. I refuse to let it go, let her down. The SS break up their picnic to relieve themselves or to smoke, and I slip out a side door.

I can smell manure and apple blossoms and German tobacco.

The grass is damp and cool. On the other side of a stucco fence, I see a garden: small lettuce heads, vines of beans, the feathery green plumes of carrot tops. I can taste the carrots as if I've already picked them, crisp and earthy. Climbing the wall isn't hard. I skin my knees a little as I shimmy over the top, and the bright spots of blood feel like fresh air on my skin, like a good thing deep down surfacing. I'm giddy. I grab the carrot tops and pull, the sound like a seam ripping as the earth releases the roots. They're heavy in my hands. Clumps of dirt dangle from the roots. Even the dirt smells like a feast—like seeds—every possible thing contained there. I scale the wall again, dirt raining onto my knees. I picture Magda's face as she bites into the first fresh vegetable we've eaten in a year. I have done a daring thing and it has borne fruit. This is what I want Magda to see, more than a meal, more than nutrients dissolving into her blood: simply, hope. I jump to earth again.

But I'm not alone. A man stares down at me. He clutches a gun. He's a German Wehrmacht soldier. Worse than the gun are his eyes, punitive eyes. *How dare you?* his eyes say. *I'll teach you to obey.* He pushes me down to my knees. He cocks the gun and points it at my chest. *Please, please, please, please.* I pray like I did with Mengele. *Please help him to not kill me.* I'm shivering. The carrots knock against my leg. He puts the gun down for a brief second, then raises it again. *Click. Click.* Worse than the fear of death is the feeling of being locked in and powerless, of not knowing what will happen in the next breath. He yanks me to my feet and turns me toward the building where Magda sleeps. He uses the butt of his gun to shove me inside.

"Pissing," he says to the guard inside, and they chuckle crassly. I hold the carrots folded in my dress.

Magda won't wake up at first. I have to put the carrot in her palm before she'll open her eyes. She eats so quickly that she bites the inside of her cheek. When she thanks me, she cries.

The SS shout us awake in the morning. Time to march again. I am starving and hollow, and I think I must have dreamed the carrots, but Magda shows me a handful of greens she has tucked in a pocket for later. They have wilted. They're scraps that in a former life we would have thrown away or fed to the goose in the attic, but now they appear enchanted, like a pot in a fairy tale that magically fills with gold. The drooping, browning carrot tops are proof of a secret power. I shouldn't have risked picking them, but I did. I shouldn't have survived, but I did. The "shoulds" aren't important. They aren't the only kind of governance. There's a different principle, a different authority at work. We are skeletal. We are so sick and undernourished that we can barely walk, much less march, much less work. And yet the carrots make me feel strong. *If I survive today, tomorrow I will be free.* I sing the chant in my head.

We line up in rows for the count. I'm still singing to myself. Just as we're about to head out into the chilly morning for another day of horrors, there's a commotion at the door. The SS guard shouts in German, and another man shouts back, pushing his way into the room. My breath catches, and I grab Magda's elbow so that I don't fall over. It's the man from the garden. He's looking sternly around the room.

"Where is the girl who dared to break the rules?" he demands.

I shake. I can't calm my body. He's back for revenge. He wants to mete out punishment publicly. Or he feels he must. Someone has learned of his inexplicable kindness to me, and now he must pay for *his* risk. He must pay for his risk by making me pay for mine. I quake, almost unable to breathe I'm so afraid. I am trapped. I know how close I am to death.

"Where is the little criminal?" he asks again.

He will spot me any second. Or he will spy the carrot tops poking out of Magda's coat. I can't bear the suspense of waiting for him to recognize me. I drop to the ground and crawl toward him. Magda hisses at me, but it's too late. I crouch at his feet. I see the mud on his boots, the grain of the wood on the floor.

"You," he says. He sounds disgusted. I close my eyes. I wait for him to kick me. I wait for him to shoot.

Something heavy drops near my feet. A stone? Will he stone me to death, the slow way?

No. It's bread. A small loaf of dark rye bread.

"You must have been very hungry to do what you did," he says. His eyes are my father's eyes. Green. And full of relief.

Chapter 9

THE STAIRS OF DEATH

We march for days or weeks again. Since Auschwitz, we have been kept in Germany, but one day we come to the Austrian border, where we wait to cross. The guards gossip as we stand in the interminable lines that have become for me the illusion of order, the illusion that one thing naturally follows another. It is a relief to stand still. I listen to the conversation between the guards. President Roosevelt has died, they are saying. Truman is left to carry out the rest of the war. How strange to hear that in the world outside our purgatory, things change. A new course is determined. These events occur so far from our daily existence that it is a shock to realize that now, even right now, someone is making a choice about me. Not about me specifically. I have no name. But someone with authority is making a decision that will determine what happens to me. North, south, east, or west? Germany or Austria? What should be done with the surviving Jews before the war is over?

"When the war ends . . . ," a guard says. He doesn't finish the thought. This is the kind of future talk that Eric and I once entertained. *After the war* . . . If I concentrate in just the right way, can I figure out if he still lives? I pretend that I'm waiting outside a train station where I will buy a ticket, but I have only one chance to figure out the city where I am to meet him. Prague? Vienna? Düsseldorf? Prešov? Paris? I reach into my pocket, feeling reflexively for my passport. *Eric, my sweet love, I am on my way.* A female border guard shouts at me and Magda in German and points us to a different line. I start to move. Magda stays still. The guard shouts again. Magda won't move, won't respond. Is she delirious? Why won't she follow me? The guard yells in Magda's face, and Magda shakes her head.

"I don't understand," Magda says to the guard in Hungarian. Of course she understands. We're both fluent in German.

"Yes, you do!" the guard shouts.

"I don't understand," Magda repeats. Her voice is completely neutral. Her shoulders are straight and tall. Am I missing something? Why is she pretending not to understand? There is nothing to be gained from defiance. Has she lost her mind? The two continue to argue. Except Magda isn't arguing. She is only repeating, flatly, calmly, that she doesn't understand, she doesn't understand. The guard loses control. She smacks Magda's face with the butt of her gun. She beats her again across the shoulders. She hits and hits until Magda topples over and the guard gestures to me and another girl to drag her away with us.

Magda is bruised and coughing, but her eyes shine. "I said no!"

she says. "I said no." For her, it is a marvelous beating. It is proof of her power. She held her ground while the guard lost control. Magda's civil disobedience makes her feel like the author of choice, not the victim of fate.

But the power Magda feels is short-lived. Soon we are marching again, toward a place worse than any we have yet seen.

We arrive at Mauthausen. It's an all-male concentration camp at a quarry where prisoners are made to hack and carry granite that will be used to build Hitler's fantasy city, a new capital for Germany, a new Berlin. I see nothing but stairs and bodies. The stairs are white stone and stretch up and up ahead of us, as though we could walk them to the sky. The bodies are everywhere, in heaps. Bodies crooked and splayed like pieces of broken fence. Bodies so skeletal and disfigured and tangled that they barely have a human shape. We stand in a line on the white stairs. The Stairs of Death, they are called. We are waiting on the stairs for another selection, we presume, that will point us to death or more work. Rumors shudder down the line. The inmates at Mauthausen, we learn, have to carry 110-pound blocks of stone from the quarry below up the 186 stairs, running in line. I picture my ancestors, the pharaoh's slaves in Egypt, bent under the weight of stones. Here on the Stairs of Death, we're told, when you're carrying a stone, running up the stairs, and someone in front of you trips or collapses, you are the next to fall, and on, and on, until the whole line buckles into a heap. If you survive, it's worse, we hear. You have to stand along a wall at the edge of a cliff. *Fallschirmspringerwand*, it's called—the

Parachutists' Wall. At gunpoint, you choose: Will you be shot to death, or will you push the inmate beside you off the cliff?

"Just push me," Magda says. "If it comes to that."

"Me too," I say. I would rather fall a thousand times than see my sister shot. We are too weak and starved to say this out of politeness. We say this out of love, but also out of self-preservation. Don't give me another heavy thing to carry. Let me fall among the stones.

I weigh less, much less, than the rocks the inmates lift up the Stairs of Death. I am so light I could drift like a leaf or a feather. Down, down. I could fall now. I could just fall backward instead of taking the next step up. I think I am empty now. There is no heaviness to hold me to the earth. I am about to indulge this fantasy of weightlessness, of releasing the burden of being alive, when someone ahead of me in line breaks the spell.

"There's the crematorium," she says.

I look up. We have been away from the death camps for so many months that I have forgotten how matter-of-factly the chimneys rise. In a way, they are reassuring. To feel death's proximity, death's imminence, in the straight stack of brick, to see the chimney that is a bridge, that will house your passage from flesh to air—to consider yourself already dead—makes a certain kind of sense.

And yet, as long as that chimney produces smoke, I have something to fight against. I have a purpose. "We die in the morning," the rumors announce. I can feel resignation tugging at me like gravity, an inevitable and constant force.

Night falls, and we sleep on the stairs. Why have they waited so long to begin the selection? My courage wavers. *We die in the morning. In the morning we die.* Did my mother know what was about to happen when she joined the line of children and the elderly? When she saw Magda and me pointed a different way? Did she fight death? Did she accept it? Did she remain oblivious until the end? Does it matter, when you go, if you are aware that you are dying? *We die in the morning. In the morning we die.* I hear the rumor, the certainty, repeat as though it is echoing off the quarry rock. Have we really been marched these many hundreds of miles only to vanish?

I want to organize my mind. I don't want my last thoughts to be cliché ones or despondent ones. *What's the point? What has it all meant?* I don't want my last thoughts to be a replaying of the horrors we've seen. I want to feel alive. I want to savor what aliveness is. I think of Eric's voice and his lips. I try to conjure thoughts that might still have the power to make me tingle. *I'll never forget your eyes. I'll never forget your hands.* That's what I want to remember—warmth in my chest, a flush across my skin—though "remember" isn't the right word. I want to enjoy my body while I still have one. An eternity ago, in Kassa, my mother forbade me to read Émile Zola's *Nana*, but I snuck it into the bathroom and read it in secret. If I die tomorrow, I will die a virgin. Why have I had a body at all, never to know it completely? So much of my life has been a mystery. How the red streaks on my white skirt surprised me when my period came. How my mother slapped me. How no one in my life before the camps, not my mother or sisters or teachers or coaches or friends, had ever explained anything about my anatomy. Now, thanks to my conversation with Esther in the barracks that night, I know there is something men have that women don't. I'd never seen my father naked, but I'd felt that part of Eric pressing against me when he held me. He had never asked me to touch it, had never acknowledged his body. I had liked the feeling that his body—and my own—were mysteries waiting to be uncovered, something that caused an energy to shoot between us when we touched.

Now it was a mystery I would never solve. I had experienced little stars of desire but would now never feel their fulfillment, the whole promised galaxy of light. I cry about it now, on the Stairs of Death. It is terrible to lose, to have lost, all the known things: mother, father, sister, boyfriend, country, home. Why do I have to lose the things I don't know too? Why do I have to lose the future? My potential? The children I'll never mother? The wedding dress my father will never make? *I'm going to die a virgin.* I don't want this to be my last thought. I should think about God.

I try to picture an immovable power. Magda has lost her faith. She and many others. "I can't believe in a God who would let this happen," they say. I understand what they mean. And yet I've never found it difficult to see that it isn't God who is killing us in gas chambers, in ditches, on cliff sides, on 186 white stairs. God doesn't run the death camps. People do. But here is the horror again, and I don't want to indulge it. I picture God as being like a dancing child. Sprightly and innocent and *curious.* I must be also if I am to be close to God now. I want to keep alive the part of me that feels wonder, that *wonders*, until the very end. I wonder if anyone knows that I am here, knows what's going on, that there is such a place as an Auschwitz, a Mauthausen? I wonder if my parents can see me now. I wonder if Eric can. I wonder what a man looks like naked. There are men all around me. Men no longer living. It wouldn't hurt their pride anymore for me to look. The worse transgression would be to relinquish my curiosity, I convince myself.

I leave Magda sleeping on the stairs and crawl to the muddy hillside where the corpses are piled. I won't undress anyone still in clothes. I won't tamper with the dead. But if a man has fallen, I will look.

I see a man, his legs askew. They don't seem to belong to the same body, but I can make out the place where the legs are joined. I see hair like mine, dark, coarse, and a little appendage. It's like a little mushroom, a tender thing that pushes out of the dirt. How strange that women's parts are all tucked away and men's are exposed, so vulnerable. I feel satisfied. I won't die ignorant of the biology that made me.

At daybreak, the line starts to move. We don't talk much. Some wail. Some pray. Mostly we are private in our dread or regret or resignation or relief. I don't tell Magda what I saw the night before. This line is moving quickly. There won't be much time. I try to remember the constellations I used to recognize in the night sky. I try to remember the taste of my mother's bread.

"Dicuka," Magda says, but it takes me a few hollow breaths

to recognize my name. We've reached the top of the stairs. The selection officer is just ahead. Everyone is being sent in the same direction. This isn't a selection line. It's an ushering. It really is the end. They've waited until morning to send us all to death. Should we make a promise to each other? An apology? What is there that must be said? Five girls ahead of us now. What should I say to my sister? Two girls.

And then the line stops. We're led toward a crowd of SS guards by a gate.

"If you try to run, you'll be shot!" they shout at us. "If you fall behind, you'll be shot."

We have been saved again. Inexplicably.

We march.

This is the Death March, from Mauthausen to Gunskirchen. It is the shortest distance we have been forced to walk, but we are so weakened by then that only one hundred out of the two thousand of us will survive. Magda and I cling to each other, determined to stay together, to stay upright. Each hour, hundreds of girls fall into the ditches on either side of the road. Too weak or too ill to keep moving, they're killed on the spot. We are like the head of a dandelion gone to seed and blown by the wind, only a few white tufts remaining. Hunger is my only name.

Every part of me is in pain; every part of me is numb. I can't walk another step. I ache so badly I can't feel myself move. I am just a circuitry of pain, a signal that feeds back on itself. I don't know that I have stumbled until I feel the arms of Magda and Lily and Marta lifting me. They have laced their fingers together to form a human chair.

"You shared your bread," Lily says.

The words don't mean anything to me. When have I ever tasted bread? But then a memory rises up. Our first night at Auschwitz. Mengele ordering the music and Mengele ordering me to dance. This body danced. This mind dreamed of the opera house. This body ate that bread. I am the one who had the thought that night and who thinks it again now: Mengele killed my mother; Mengele let me live. Now a girl I shared a crust with nearly a year ago has recognized me. She uses her last strength to interlace her fingers with Magda's and those of the other girls and lift me up into the air. In a way, Mengele allowed this moment to happen. He didn't kill any of us that night or any night after. He gave us bread.

Chapter 10

TO CHOOSE A BLADE OF GRASS

There is always a worse hell. That is our reward for living. When we stop marching, we are at Gunskirchen Lager. It's a sub-camp of Mauthausen, a few wooden buildings in a marshy forest near a village, a camp built to house a few hundred slave laborers, where eighteen thousand are crowded now. It is not a death camp. There are no gas chambers here, no crematoria. But there is no doubt that we have been sent here to die.

It is already hard to tell who is living and who is dead. Disease passes into and between our bodies. Typhus. Dysentery. White lice. Open sores. Flesh upon flesh. Living and rotting. A horse's carcass half-gnawed. Eat it raw. Who needs a knife to cut the flesh? Just gnaw it away from the bone. You sleep three deep, in the crowded wooden structures or on the bare ground. If someone below you dies, keep sleeping. No strength to haul the dead away. There's a girl doubled over in hunger. There's a foot, black, rotted through. We have been herded into the dank, thick woods to be killed in a giant blaze, all of us lit on fire. The whole place is rigged with dynamite. We wait for the explosion that will consume us in its flame. Until the big blast, there are other hazards: starvation, fever, disease. There is only one twenty-hole latrine for the entire camp. If you can't wait your turn to defecate, they shoot you right there, where your waste has pooled. Trash fires smolder. The earth is a mud pit, and if you can find the strength to walk, your feet spin in a pulp that is part mud, part shit. It is five or six months since we left Auschwitz.

Magda flirts. That is her answer to death's beckoning. She meets a Frenchman, a guy from Paris, who lived before the war on Rue de something, an address I tell myself I won't ever forget. Even in the depths of this horror there is chemistry, person to person, that gallop in the throat, that brightening. I watch them talk as though they are seated at a summer café, little plates clinking between them. This is what the living do. We use our sacred pulse as a flint against fear. Don't ruin your spirit. Send it up like a torch. Tell the Frenchman your name and tuck his address away, savor it, chew it slowly like bread.

In just a few days at Gunskirchen, I become a person who cannot walk. I sense that I have reached the end of my reserves. I lie out in the heavy air, my body entwined with strangers' bodies, all of us in a heap, some already dead, some long dead, some, like me, barely alive. I see things I know aren't real. I see them all mixed in with the things that *are* real but shouldn't be. My mother reads to me. Scarlett cries, *"I've loved something that doesn't really exist."* My father throws me a petit four. Klara starts the Mendelssohn violin concerto. She plays by the window so that a passerby will notice her, lift a face toward her, so she can beckon for the attention she craves and can't ask for outright. This is what the living do. We set strings vibrating with our needs.

Here in hell, I watch a man eat human flesh. Could I do it? For the sake of my own life, could I put my mouth around the skin left hanging on a dead person's bones and chew? I have seen flesh defiled in unforgivable cruelty. A boy tied to a tree while the SS officers shot his foot, his hand, his arms, an ear—an innocent child used as target practice. Or the pregnant woman who somehow made it to Auschwitz without being killed outright. When she went into labor, the SS tied her legs together. I've never seen agony like hers. But it's watching a starving person eat a dead person's flesh that makes the bile rise in me, that makes my vision black. I cannot do it. And yet I must eat. I must eat or I will die. Out of the trampled mud grows grass. I stare at the blades. I see their different lengths and shades. I will eat grass. I will choose this blade of grass over that one. I will occupy my mind with the choice. This is what it means to choose. To eat or not eat. To eat grass or to eat flesh. To eat this blade or that one. Mostly we sleep. There is nothing to drink. I lose all sense of time. I am often asleep. Even when I am awake, I struggle to remain conscious.

Once I see Magda crawling back to me with a can in her hand, a can that glints in the sun. A can of sardines. The Red Cross, in its neutrality, has been allowed to deliver aid to prisoners, and Magda has huddled in a line and been handed a can of sardines. But there's no way to open it. It's just a new flavor of cruelty. Even a good intention, a good deed, becomes futility. My sister is dying slowly of starvation; my sister holds food in her hand. She clutches the tin the way she clutched her hair once, trying to hold on to herself. An unopenable can of fish is the most human part of her now. We are the dead and the near dead. I can't tell which I am.

I am aware at the corners of my consciousness of day trading places with night. When I open my eyes, I don't know if I have slept or fainted, or for how long. I don't have the capacity to ask, *How long?* Sometimes I can feel that I am breathing. Sometimes I try to move my head to look for Magda. Sometimes I can't think of her name.

Cries break me out of a sleep that resembles death. The cries must be death's herald. I wait for the promised explosion, for the promised heat. I keep my eyes closed and wait to burn. But there's no explosion. There's no flame. I open my eyes, and I can see jeeps rolling slowly in through the pine forest that obscures the camp from the road and from the sky. "The Americans have arrived! The Americans are here!" This is what the feeble are shouting. The jeeps look wavy and blurry, as if I am watching them through water or in an intense heat. Could this be a collective hallucination? Someone is singing "When the Saints Go Marching In." I see men in fatigues. I see flags with stars and stripes—American flags, I realize. I see flags emblazoned with the number 71. I see an

American handing cigarettes to inmates, who are so hungry they eat them, paper and all. I watch from a tangle of bodies. I can't tell which legs are my legs. "Are there any living here?" the Americans call in German. "Raise your hand if you are alive." I try to move my fingers to signal that I am alive. A soldier walks so near to me that I can see the streaks of mud on his pants. I can smell his sweat. *Here I am*, I want to call. *I'm here*. I have no voice. He scours the bodies. His eyes pass over me without recognition. He holds a piece of dirty cloth to his face. "Raise your hand if you can hear me," he says. He barely moves the cloth away from his mouth when he speaks. I work to find my fingers. *You'll never get out of here alive*, they've said: the *kapo* who ripped out my earrings, the SS officer with the tattoo gun who didn't want to waste the ink, the forewoman in the thread factory, the SS who shot us down on the long, long march. This is how it feels for them to be right.

The soldier shouts something in English. Someone outside my field of vision yells back. They're leaving.

And then a patch of light explodes on the ground. Here's the fire. At last. I am surprised that it makes no noise. The soldiers turn. My numb body suddenly flushes hot—from flame, I think, or fever. But no. There is no fire. The gleam of light isn't fire at all. It is the sun colliding with Magda's sardine can! Whether on purpose or by accident, she has arrested the soldiers' attention with a tin of fish. They are returning. We have one more chance. If I can dance in my mind, I can make my body be seen. I close my eyes and concentrate, raising my hands above my head in an imaginary arabesque. I hear the soldiers yell again, one to the other. One is very close to me. I keep my eyes locked shut and continue my dance. I imagine that I am dancing with him. That he lifts me over his head like Romeo did in the barracks with Mengele. That there is love and it springs out of war. That there is death and always, always its opposite.

And now I can feel my hand. I know it is my hand because the soldier is touching it. I open my eyes. I see that his wide, dark hand circles my fingers. He presses something into my hand. Beads. Colorful beads. Red, brown, green, yellow.

"Food," the soldier says. He looks into my eyes. His skin is the darkest I have ever seen, his lips thick, his eyes deep brown. He helps me lift my hand to my mouth. He helps me release the beads onto my dry tongue. Saliva gathers, and I taste something sweet. I taste chocolate. I remember the name of this flavor. *Always keep a little something sweet in your pocket*, my father said. Here is the sweetness.

But Magda? Has she been discovered too? I don't have words yet, or a voice. I can't stammer a thank-you. I can't form the syllables of my sister's name. I can barely swallow the little candies the soldier has given me. I can barely think of anything other than the desire for more food. Or a drink of water. His attention is occupied now with getting me out of the pile of bodies. He has to pull the dead away from me. They are slack in the face, slack in their limbs. As skeletal as they are, they are heavy, and he grimaces and strains as he lifts them. Sweat streaks his face. He coughs at the stench. He adjusts the cloth over his mouth. Who knows how long the dead have been dead? Maybe only a breath or two separates them from me. I don't know how to speak my thankfulness. But I feel it prickling all across my skin.

He lifts me now and deposits me on the ground, on my back, at a slight distance from the dead bodies. I can see the sky in pieces between the treetops. I feel the humid air on my face, the dampness of the muddy grass beneath me. I let my mind rest in sensation. I picture my mother's long coiled hair, my father's top hat and mustache. Everything I feel and have ever felt stems from them, from the union that made me. They rocked me in their arms. They made me a child of the earth. I remember Magda's story about my birth. "You helped me," my mother cried to her mother. "You helped me."

And now Magda is beside me in the grass. She holds her can of sardines. We have survived the final selection. We are alive. We are together. We are free.

Chapter 11

MY LIBERATOR, MY ASSAILANT

When I permitted myself to imagine a moment like this—the end of my imprisonment, the end of the war—I imagined a joy blooming in my chest. I imagined yelling in my fullest voice, "I AM FREE! I AM FREE!" But now I have no voice. We are a silent river, a current of the freed that flows from the Gunskirchen graveyard toward the nearest town. I ride on a makeshift cart. The wheels squeak. I can barely stay conscious. There is no joy or relief in this freedom. It's a slow walk out of a forest. It's a dazed face. It's being barely alive and returning to sleep. It's the danger of gorging on sustenance. The danger of the wrong kind of sustenance. Freedom is sores and lice and typhus and carved-out bellies and listless eyes.

I am aware of Magda walking beside me. Of pain throughout my body as the cart jolts. For more than a year I have not had the luxury of thinking about what hurts or doesn't hurt. I have been able to think only about how to keep up with the others, how to stay one step ahead, to get a little food here, to walk fast enough, to never stop, to stay alive, to not be left behind. Now that the danger is gone, the pain within and the suffering around me turn awareness into hallucination. A silent movie. A march of skeletons. Most of us are too physically ruined to walk. We lie on carts. We lean on sticks. Our uniforms are filthy and worn, so ragged and tattered that they hardly cover our skin. Our skin hardly covers our bones. We are an anatomy lesson. Elbows, knees, ankles, cheeks, knuckles, ribs jut out like questions. What are we now? Our bones look obscene; our eyes are caverns, blank, dark, empty. Hollow faces. Blue-black fingernails. We are trauma in motion. We are a slow-moving parade of ghouls. We stagger as we walk; our carts roll over the cobblestones. Row on row, we fill the square in Wels, Austria. Townspeople stare at us from windows. We are frightening. No one speaks. We choke the square with our silence. Townspeople run into their homes. Children cover their eyes. We have lived through hell only to become someone else's nightmare.

The important thing is to eat and drink. But not too much, not too fast. It is possible to overdose on food. To die from eating too much. Some of us can't help it. Restraint has dissolved along with our muscle mass, our flesh. We have starved for so long. Now it's deadly both to sustain and to end hunger. A blessing, then, that the strength I need to chew returns to me only intermittently. A blessing that the GIs have little food to offer, mostly candy, those little beads of color, M&M's, we learn.

No one wants to house us. Hitler has been dead for less than a week. Germany has not yet officially surrendered. The violence is waning across Europe, but it is still wartime. Food and hope are scarce for everyone. And we survivors, we former captives, are still the enemy to some. Parasites. Vermin. The war does not end anti-Semitism. The GIs bring Magda and me to a house where a German family lives, a mother, father, grandmother, three children. This is where we will live until we are strong enough to travel. Be careful, the Americans warn us in broken German. There's no peace yet. Anything could happen.

The parents move all of the family's possessions into a bedroom, and the father makes a show of locking the door. The children take turns staring at us and then run to hide their faces behind their mother's skirt. We are containers for their fascination and their fear. I am used to the blank-eyed, automatic cruelty of the SS, or their incongruous cheer—their delight in power. I am used to the way they lift themselves up, to feel big, to heighten their sense of purpose and control. The way the children look at us is worse. We are an offense to innocence. That's the way the children look at us—as though we are the transgressors. Their shock is more bitter than hate.

The soldiers bring us to the room where we will sleep. It's the nursery. We are the orphans of war. They lift me into a wooden crib. I am that small; I weigh seventy pounds. I can't walk on my own. I am a baby. I barely think in language. I think in terms of pain, of need. I would cry to be held, but there's no one to hold me. Magda curls into a ball on the little bed.

A noise outside our door splinters my sleep. Even rest is fragile. I am afraid all the time. I am afraid of what has already happened. And of what could happen. Sounds in the dark bring back the image of my mother tucking Klara's caul into her coat, my father gazing back at our apartment on the early morning of our eviction. As the past replays, I lose my home and my parents all over again. I stare at the wooden slats of the crib and try to soothe myself back to sleep, or at least into calm.

But the noises persist. Crashes and stomps. And then the door flies open. Two GIs careen into the room. They stumble over each other, over a little shelf. Lamplight strains into the dark room. One of the men points at me and laughs and grabs his crotch. Magda isn't there. I don't know where she is, if she is close enough to hear me if I scream, if she is cowering somewhere, as afraid as I am. I hear my mother's voice. *Don't you dare lose your virginity before you're married*, she would lecture us, before I even knew what virginity was. I didn't have to. I understood the threat. Don't ruin yourself. Don't disappoint. Now rough handling could do more than tarnish me; it could kill me. I am that brittle. But it's not just dying or more pain that I fear. I'm afraid of losing my mother's respect.

The soldier shoves his friend back to the door to keep watch. He comes at me, cooing absurdly, his voice grainy, dislocated. His sweat and the alcohol on his breath smell sharp, like mold. I have to keep him away from me. There is nothing to throw. I can't even sit. I try to scream, but my voice is just a warble. The soldier at the door is laughing. But then he isn't. He speaks harshly. I can't understand English, but I know he says something about a baby. The other soldier leans against the crib rail. His hand gropes toward his waist. He will use me. Crush me. He pulls out his gun. He waves it crazily like a torch. I wait for his hands to clamp down on me. But he moves away instead. He moves toward the door, toward his friend. The door clicks shut. I'm alone in the dark.

I can't sleep. I'm sure the soldier will return. And where is Magda? Has some other soldier taken her? She is emaciated, but her body is in much better shape than mine, and there is still a hint of her feminine figure. To settle my mind, I try to organize what I know of men, of the human palette: Eric, tender and optimistic; my father, disappointed in himself and circumstance, sometimes defeated, sometimes making the best of it, finding the little joys; Dr. Mengele, lascivious and controlled; the Wehrmacht who caught me with the carrots fresh from the ground, punitive but merciful, then kind; the GI who pulled me from the heap of bodies at Gunskirchen, determined and brave; and now this new flavor, this new shade. A liberator, but an assailant, his presence heavy but also void. A big dark blank, as though his humanity has vacated his body. Some part of me knows that the man who nearly raped me, who might still come back to do what he started to do, saw horror too. Like me, he is probably caught in its web, trying to chase it away, to push it to the margins. Lost in the darkness, he almost became it.

He returns in the morning. I know it is him because he still reeks of booze, because fear has made me memorize the map of his face even though I saw it in semidarkness. I hug my knees and whimper. I sound like an animal. I can't stop. It's a keening, droning noise, part insect. He kneels by the crib. He is weeping. He repeats three syllables. I don't know what they mean. He hands me a cloth sack. It's too heavy for me to lift, so he empties it for me, spilling the contents—small tins of army rations—onto the mattress. He shows me the pictures on the cans. He points and talks, a crazy maître d' explaining the menu, inviting me to choose my next meal. I can't understand a word he says. I study the pictures. He pries open a can and feeds me with a spoon. It's ham with something sweet, raisins. If my father hadn't shared his secret packages of pork, I might not know the taste of it—though Hungarians would never pair ham with anything sweet. I keep opening my mouth, receiving another bite. Of course I forgive him. I am starving, and he brings me food to eat.

He comes back every day. Magda is well enough to flirt again, and I assume that he makes a point of visiting this house because he enjoys her attention. But day after day, he barely notices her. He comes for me. I am what he needs to resolve. Maybe he's doing penance for his near assault. Or maybe he needs to prove to himself that hope and innocence can be resurrected, his, mine, the world's—that a broken girl can walk again. The GI lifts me out of the crib and holds my hands and coaxes me a step at a time around the room. The pain in my upper back feels like a burning coal when I try to move. I concentrate on shifting my weight from one foot to the other, trying to feel the exact moment when the weight transfers. My hands reach overhead, holding on to his fingers. I pretend he is my father, my father who wished I'd been a boy and then loved me anyway. *You'll be the best-dressed girl in town*, he told me over and over again. When I think of my father, the heat pulls out of my back and glows in my chest. There is pain and there is love. A baby knows these two shades of the world, and I am relearning them too.

Magda is physically better off than I am, and she tries to put our lives in order. One day when the German family is out of the house, Magda opens closets until she finds dresses for us to wear. She sends letters—to Klara, to our mother's brother in Budapest, to our mother's sister in Miskolc—to discover who might still be living, to discover where to build a life when it's time to leave Wels. I can't remember how to write my own name. Much less an address. A sentence. *Are you there?*

One day the GI brings paper and pencils. We start with the alphabet. He writes a capital *A*. A lowercase *a*. Capital *B*. Lowercase *b*. He gives me the pencil and nods. Can I make any letters? He wants me to try. He wants to see how far I've regressed, how much I remember. I can write *C* and *c*. *D* and *d*. I remember! He encourages me. He cheers me on. *E* and *e*. *F* and *f*. But then I falter. I know that *G* comes next, but I can't picture it, can't think how to form it on the page.

One day he brings a radio. He plays the happiest music I have ever heard. It's buoyant. It propels you. I hear horns. They insist that you move. Their shimmer isn't seduction—it's deeper than that; it's invitation, impossible to refuse. The GI and his friends show Magda and me the dances that go along with the sound—jitterbug, boogie-woogie. The men pair up like ballroom dancers. Even the way they hold their arms is new to me—it's ballroom style but loose, pliable. It's informal but not sloppy. How do they keep themselves so taut with energy and yet so flexible? So *ready*? Their bodies live out whatever the music sets in motion. I want to dance like that. I want to let my muscles remember.

Magda goes to take a bath one morning and returns to the room shaking. Her hair is wet, her clothes half-off. She rocks on the bed with her eyes closed. I've been sleeping on the bed while she bathed—I'm too big for the crib now—and I don't know whether or not she knows I am awake.

It's been more than a month since liberation. Magda and I have spent almost every hour of the last forty days together in this room. We have regained the use of our bodies. We have regained the ability to talk and to write and even to try to dance. We can talk about Klara, about our hope that somewhere she is alive and trying to find us. But we can't talk about what we have endured.

Maybe in our silence we are trying to create a sphere that is free from our trauma. Wels is a limbo life, but presumably a new life beckons. Maybe we are trying to give each other and ourselves a blank room in which to build the future. We don't want to sully the room with images of violence and loss. We want to be able to see something besides death. And so we tacitly agree not to talk about anything that will rupture the bubble of survival.

Now my sister is trembling and hurting. If I tell her I am

awake, if I ask her what is wrong, if I become witness to her breakdown, she won't have to be all alone with whatever is making her shake. But if I pretend I am asleep, I can preserve for her a mirror that doesn't reflect back this new pain; I can be a selective mirror. I can shine back at her the things she wants to cultivate and leave everything else invisible.

In the end, I don't have to decide what to do. She begins to speak.

"Before I leave this house, I will get my revenge," she vows.

We rarely see the family whose house we occupy, but her quiet, bitter anger compels me to imagine the worst. I picture the father coming into the bathroom while she undressed. "Did he . . . ?" I stammer.

"No." Her breath is jagged. "I tried to use the soap. The room started spinning."

"Are you ill?"

"No. Yes. I don't know."

"Do you have a fever?"

"No. It's the soap, Dicu. I couldn't touch it. A sort of panic came over me."

"No one hurt you?"

"No. It was the soap. You know what they say. They say it's made from people. From the ones they killed." I don't know if it's true. But this close to Gunskirchen? Maybe.

"I still want to kill a German mother," Magda says. I remember all the miles we walked in winter when this was her fantasy, her refrain. "I could do it, you know."

There are different ways to keep yourself going. I will have to find my own way to live with what has happened. I don't know what it is yet.

One day the GI and his friends come to tell us we'll be leaving Wels, that the Russians are helping transport the survivors home. They come to say goodbye. They bring the radio. Glenn Miller's "In the Mood" comes on, and we let loose. With my painful back, I can barely manage the steps, but in my mind, in my spirit, we are spinning tops. Slow, slow, fast-fast, slow. Slow, slow, fast-fast, slow. I can do it too—keep my arms and legs loose but not limp. Glenn Miller. Duke Ellington. I repeat the big names in big band over and over. The GI leads me in a careful turn, a tiny dip, a breakaway. I am still so weak, but I can feel the potential in my body, all the things it will be possible to say with it when I have healed. Dancing to Glenn Miller six weeks after liberation, with my sister who is alive and the GI who almost raped me but didn't, I feel the part of me that is returning, that is coming into its own. The limbs and the life I can grow into again.

During the several hours' train ride from Wels to Vienna, through Russian-occupied Austria, I scratch at the rash, from lice or rubella, that still covers my body. Home. We are going home. In two more days we will be home! And yet it is impossible to feel the joy of our homecoming uncoupled from the devastation of loss. I know my mother is dead, and surely my father and grandparents too. To go home without them is to lose them again. *Maybe Klara*, I allow myself to hope. *Maybe Eric.* When I was a prisoner, hope required imagination. Now it requires faith.

In the seat next to ours, two brothers sit. They are survivors too. Orphans. From Kassa, like us! Lester and Imre, they are called. Their father was shot in the back as he walked between them on the Death March.

"We have one another," they say. "We are lucky, lucky."

Lester and Imre, Magda and me. We are the anomalies. The Nazis didn't just murder millions of people. They murdered families. And now, beside the incomprehensible roster of the missing and the dead, our lives go on. We stare out the windows of the train, looking at empty fields, broken bridges, and, in some places, the fragile beginnings of crops. The mood in the towns we pass through isn't of relief or celebration—it's a teeth-clenched atmosphere of uncertainty and hunger. The war is over, but it's not over.

"Do I have ugly lips?" Magda asks as we near the outskirts of Vienna. She is studying her reflection in the window glass, superimposed over the landscape.

"Why, are you planning to use them?" I joke with her, I try to coax out that relentlessly teasing part of her. I reach for my fantasies, that Eric is alive somewhere, that soon I will be a postwar bride under a makeshift veil. That I will be together with my beloved forever, never alone.

"I'm serious," she says. "Tell me the truth."

Her anxiety reminds me of our first day at Auschwitz, when she stood naked with her shaved head, gripping strands of her hair.

Maybe she condenses the huge global fears about what will happen next into more specific and personal fears—the fear that she is not attractive enough to find a man, the fear that her lips are ugly. Or maybe her questions are tangled up in deeper uncertainty—about her essential worth.

"What's wrong with your lips?" I ask.

"Mama hated them. Someone on the street complimented my eyes once and she said, 'Yes, she's got beautiful eyes, but look at her thick lips.'"

Survival is black-and-white, no "buts" can intrude when you are fighting for your life. Now the "buts" come rushing in. We have bread to eat. *Yes, but we are penniless.* You are gaining weight. *Yes, but my heart is heavy.* You are alive. *Yes, but my mother is dead.*

Lester and Imre decide to stay on in Vienna for a few days; they promise to look for us at home. Magda and I board another train, which will carry us eight hours northwest to Prague. A man blocks the entrance to the train car. "*Nasa lude,*" he sneers. *Our people.* He is Slovak. The Jews must ride on top of the train car.

"The Nazis lost," Magda mutters, "but it's the same as before."

There is no other way to get home. We climb to the top of the train car, joining ranks with the other displaced persons. We hold hands. Magda sits beside a young man named Laci Gladstein. He caresses Magda's fingers with his own, his fingers barely more than bones. We do not ask one another where we have been. Our bodies and our haunted eyes say everything there is to know. Magda leans against Laci's thin chest, searching for warmth. I am jealous of the solace they seem to find in each other, the attraction, the belonging. I am too committed to my love for Eric, to my hope that I will find him again, to seek a man's arms to hold me now. Even if I didn't carry Eric's voice with me still, I think I would be too afraid to look for comfort, for intimacy. I am skin and bones. I am covered in bugs and sores. Who would want me? Better not to risk connection and be denied, better not to have my damage confirmed. And besides, who would provide the best shelter now? Someone who knows what I have endured, a fellow survivor? Or someone who doesn't, who can help me forget? Someone who knew me before I went through hell, who can help me back to my former self? Or someone who can look at me now without always seeing what's been destroyed? *I'll never forget your eyes*, Eric told me. *I'll never forget your hands.* For more than a year I have held on to these words like a map that could lead me to freedom. But what if Eric can't face what I have become? What if we find each other and build a life, only to discover that our children are the children of ghosts?

I huddle against Magda. She and Laci talk about the future.

"I'm going to be a doctor," he says.

It's noble, a young man who, like me, was little more than dead only a month or two ago. He has lived. He will heal. He will heal others. His ambition reassures me. And it startles. He has come out of the death camps with dreams. If Eric is alive, is his yearning to be a doctor still intact? It seems an unnecessary risk. Even now that I have known starvation and atrocity, I remember the pain of lesser hurts, of a dream ruined by prejudice, of the way my coach spoke to me when she cut me from the Olympic training team. I remember my grandfather, how he retired from the Singer Sewing Machine Company and waited for his pension check. How he waited and waited, how he talked of little else. Finally, he received his first check. A week later we were evacuated to the brick factory. I don't want to dream the wrong thing.

"I have an uncle in America," Laci continues. "In Texas. I'll go there, work, save up for school."

"Maybe we'll go to America too," Magda says. She must be thinking of Aunt Matilda, in the Bronx. All around us on the top of the train car, there is talk of America, of Palestine. Why keep living in the ashes of our loss? Why keep scratching for survival in a place where we're not wanted? Soon we will learn of the restrictive immigration limits in America and Palestine. There is no haven free of limitation, of prejudice. Wherever we go, life might always be like this. Trying to ignore the fear that any minute we'll be bombed, shot, tossed in a ditch. Or at best forced to ride on top of the train, holding hands against the wind.

In Prague we are to change trains again. We say goodbye to Laci. Magda gives him our old address, Kossuth Lajos Utca #6. He promises to keep in touch. There's time before the next departure, time to stretch our legs and sit in the sun and the quiet to eat our bread. I want to find a park. I want to see green growth, flowers. I close my eyes every few steps and take in the smells of a city, the streets and sidewalks and civilian bustle. Bakeries, car exhaust, perfume. It's hard to believe that all of this existed while we were in our hell. I gaze into shop windows. It doesn't matter that I am penniless. It will matter, of course. In Košice food won't be given out for free. But at this moment I feel completely full just seeing that there are dresses and stockings to buy, jewelry, pipes, stationery. Life and commerce go on. A woman fingers the weight of a summer dress. A man admires a necklace. Things aren't important, but beauty is. Here is a city full of people who have not lost the capacity to imagine, make, and admire beautiful things. I will be a resident again—a resident of somewhere. I will run errands and buy gifts. I will stand in line at the post office. I will eat bread that I have baked. I will wear fine couture in honor of my father. I will go to the opera in honor of my mother, of how she would sit at the edge of her chair listening to Wagner, how she would weep. I will go to the symphony. And for Klara, I'll seek out every performance of Mendelssohn's violin concerto. That longing and wistfulness. The urgency as the line climbs, and then the rippling cadenza, the crashing, rising chords. And then the more sinister theme in the strings, threatening the solo violin's rising dreams. Standing on the sidewalk, I've closed my eyes so I can hear the echo of my sister's violin. Magda startles me.

"Wake up, Dicu!"

And when I open my eyes, right here in the thick of the city, near the entrance to the park, there's a concert poster advertising a performance with a solo violinist.

The picture on the poster is my sister's.

There on the paper my Klarie sits, holding her violin.

Chapter 12

IN THROUGH A WINDOW

We step off the train in Košice. Our hometown is no longer in Hungary. It is part of Czechoslovakia again. We blink into the June sun. We have no money for a taxi, no money for anything, no idea if our family's old apartment is occupied, no idea how we will find a way to live. But we are home. We are ready to search for our sister. Klara, who gave a concert in Prague only weeks ago. Klara who, somewhere, is alive.

We walk through Mestský Park, toward the center of town. People sit at outdoor tables, on benches. Children gather around the fountains. There's the clock where Sara and I watched the boys gather in expectation of meeting and flirting with us. There's the balcony of our father's shop, the gold medals blazing from the railing. *He's here!* I am so certain of it that I smell his tobacco, feel his mustache on my cheek. But the windows of the shop are dark.

We walk toward our apartment at Kossuth Lajos Utca #6, and here on the sidewalk near the place where the wagon parked before it carried us to the brick factory, a miracle occurs. Klara materializes, walking out the front door. Her hair is braided and coiled like our mother's. She carries her violin. When she sees me, she drops the violin case on the sidewalk and runs to me. She's moaning. "Dicuka, Dicuka!" she cries. She picks me up like a baby, her arms a cradle.

"Don't hug us!" Magda shrieks. "We're covered in bugs and sores!"

I think what she means is, *Dear sister, we're scarred.* She means, *Don't let what we've seen hurt you. Don't make it worse. Don't ask us what happened. Don't vanish into thin air.*

Klara rocks me and rocks me. "This is my little one!" she calls to a passing stranger. In an instant she becomes my mother. She must have seen in our faces that the position is empty and must be filled.

It has been at least a year and a half since we have seen her. She is on her way to the radio station to give a concert. We are desperate not to have her out of sight, out of touch. "Stay, stay," we beg. But she is already late. "If I don't play, we don't eat," she says. "Hurry, follow me inside." Maybe it is a blessing that there is no time to talk now. We wouldn't know how to begin. Though it must shock Klara to see us so physically ravaged, maybe that is a blessing too. There is something concrete Klara can do to express her love and relief, to point us in the direction of healing. It will take more than rest. Perhaps we will never recover. But there is something she can do right now. She brings us inside and strips off our dirty clothes. She helps us stretch out on the white sheets in the bed where our parents used to sleep. She rubs calamine lotion into the rash that covers our bodies. The rash that makes us itch and itch passes instantly from our bodies to hers so she can barely play her concert for the burning all over her skin. Our reunion is physical.

Magda and I spend at least a week in bed, naked, bodies doused in calamine. Klara doesn't ask us questions. She doesn't ask us where our mother and father are. She talks so that we don't have to. She talks so that she doesn't have to hear. Everything she tells us is phrased like a miracle. And it is miraculous. Here we are together. We are the lucky ones. There are few reunions like ours. Out of the more than fifteen thousand deportees from our hometown, we are among only seventy who have returned. Our aunt and uncle—our mother's siblings—were thrown off a bridge and drowned in the Danube, Klara tells us, blunt, matter-of-fact, but when the last remaining Jews in Hungary were rounded up, she escaped detection. She lived in her professor's house, disguised as a gentile. "One day my professor said, 'You have to learn the Bible tomorrow. You are going to start teaching it. You are going to live in a nunnery.' It seemed like the best way to keep me hidden. The convent was nearly two hundred miles from Budapest. I wore a habit. But one day a girl from the academy recognized me, and I snuck away on a train back to Budapest."

Sometime in the summer, she got a letter from our parents. It was the letter they had written while we were in the brick factory, telling Klara where we were imprisoned, that we were together, safe, that we thought we would be transferred to a work camp called Kenyérmező. I remember seeing my mother drop the letter onto the street during our evacuation from the brick factory, since there was no way to mail it. At the time I thought she had dropped it in resignation. But listening to Klara tell her story of survival, I see things differently. In releasing the letter, my mother wasn't relinquishing hope—she was kindling it. Either way, whether she dropped the letter in defeat or in hope, she took a risk. The letter pointed a finger at my sister, a blond-haired Jew hiding in Budapest. It gave her address. While we trundled in the dark toward Auschwitz, someone, a stranger, held that letter in his hand. He could have opened it. He could have turned Klara in to the *nyilas.* He could have thrown the letter away in the trash or left it in the street. But this stranger put a stamp on it and mailed it to Klara in Budapest. This is as unbelievable to me as my sister's reappearance; it's a magic trick, evidence of a lifeline that runs between us, evidence, too, that kindness still existed in the world even then. Through the dirt kicked up by three thousand pairs of feet, many of them headed straight for a chimney in Poland, our mother's letter flew. A blond-haired girl set her violin down to rip open the seal.

Klara tells another story with a happy ending. With the knowledge that we'd been evacuated to the brick factory, that we expected any day to get shipped away, to Kenyérmező or who knows where, she went to the German consulate in Budapest to demand to be sent to wherever we were. At the consulate, the doorman told her,

"Little girl, go away. Don't come in here." She wasn't going to be told no. She tried to sneak back into the building. The doorman saw her and beat her up, punching her shoulders, her arms, her stomach, her face. "Get out of here," he said again.

"He beat me up and saved my life," she tells us.

Near the end of the war, when the Russians surrounded Budapest, the Nazis became even more determined to rid the city of Jews. "We had to carry identification cards with our name, religion, picture. They were checking these cards all the time on the streets, and if they saw you were a Jew, they might kill you. I did not want to carry my card, but I was afraid I would need something to prove who I was after the war. So I decided to give mine to a girlfriend to keep for me. She lived across the harbor, so I had to cross the bridge to get there, and when I got to the bridge, the soldiers were checking identification. They said, 'Please show me who you are.' I said I had nothing, and somehow—I don't know how—they let me go across. My blond hair and blue eyes must have convinced them. I never went back to my friend's house to retrieve the card."

When you can't go in through a door, go in through a window, our mother used to say. There is no door for survival. Or recovery either. It's all windows. Latches you can't reach easily, panes too small, spaces where a body shouldn't fit. But you can't stand where you are. You must find a way.

After the German surrender, while Magda and I were recovering in Wels, Klara went to a consulate again, this time the Russian consulate, because Budapest had been liberated from Nazi control by the Red Army, and tried to learn what had become of us.

They had no information about our family, but in exchange for a free concert, they offered to help her get home to Košice. "When I played, two hundred Russians attended, and then I was brought home on top of a train. They watched over me when we stopped and slept." When she opened the door to our old apartment, everything was in disarray, our furniture and possessions looted. The rooms had been used as a stable, and the floors were covered in horse manure. While we were learning to eat, walk, and write our names in Wels, Klara began playing concerts for money and scrubbing the floors.

And now we've come. When our rashes are healed, we take turns leaving the apartment. There is only one good pair of shoes among the three of us. When it's my turn to wear the shoes, I walk slowly on the sidewalk, back and forth, still too weak to go far. A neighbor recognizes me. "I'm surprised to see you made it," he says. "You were always such a skinny little kid." I could feel triumph. Against all odds, a happy ending! But I feel guilt. Why me? Why did I make it? There is no explanation. It's a fluke. Or a mistake.

The portrait of our mother's mother still hangs on the wall. Her dark hair is parted down the middle and pulled back in a tight bun. A few curly strands feather across her smooth forehead. She doesn't smile in the picture, but her eyes are more sincere than severe. She watches us, knowing and no-nonsense. Magda talks to her portrait as our mother used to do. Sometimes she asks for help. Sometimes she mutters and rants. "Those Nazi bastards . . .

The damned *nyilas* . . ." The piano that lived against the wall under her portrait is gone. The piano was so present in our daily lives that it was almost invisible, like breath. Now its absence dominates the room. Magda rages at the empty space. With the piano gone, something in her is missing too. A piece of her identity. An outlet for her self-expression. In its absence, she finds anger. Vibrant, full voiced, willful. I admire her for it. My anger turns inward and congeals in my lungs.

Magda grows stronger as the days pass, but I am still weak. My upper back continues to ache, making it difficult to walk, and my chest is heavy with congestion. I rarely leave the house. There is one place I long to go, one person I long to ask about, but I have to get my strength back. I have to work up to the risk.

I rely on my sisters: Klara, my devoted nurse; Magda, my source of news, my connection to the greater world. One day she comes home breathless. "The piano!" she says. "I found it. It's in the coffeehouse. *Our* piano. We've got to get it back."

The coffeehouse owner won't believe that it's ours. Klara and Magda take turns pleading. They describe the family chamber music concerts in our parlor, how János Starker, Klara's cellist friend, another child prodigy from the conservatory, played a concert with Klara in our house the year of his professional debut. None of their words holds sway. Finally, Magda seeks out the piano tuner. He comes with her to the café and talks to the owner and then looks inside the piano lid to read the serial number. "Yes," he says, nodding, "this is the Elefánt piano." He gets together a crew of men to bring it back to our apartment.

Is there something inside me that can verify *my* identity, that can restore myself to myself? If such a thing existed, who would I seek out to lift the lid, read the code?

One day a package arrives from Aunt Matilda. *Valentine Avenue, the Bronx*, the return address reads. She sends tea, Crisco. We have never seen Crisco before and so have no idea that it's a butter substitute to be used for cooking and baking. We eat it plain, we spread it on bread. We reuse the tea bags again and again. How many cups can we brew with the same leaves?

I begin to make longer excursions into town. Practice excursions. Practice encounters with my life before the war. Finding Eric is the most important task. I'll start with less vital reunions and work my way up. I walk to the gymnastics studio. I'm not sure what I will say to my coach if I see her. I'm not sure how I will feel. But I have to learn how to be Edith again, Edith who survived, Edith who returned. The studio is unlocked. I climb the familiar stairs. I smell sweat and rubber, part musty, part bitter, part sweet. Younger girls are practicing on the mats and beams. Someone is practicing on the rope, another doing the splits. No one approaches me. I don't recognize anyone there, and no one seems to recognize me. I ask about my coach.

"When is she expected back?" I ask one of the new coaches.

She stares at me for a moment, then shakes her head. "She doesn't work here anymore," she says.

At first I think she's speaking in code, in euphemism. If

someone came to our apartment looking for our mother, I could say, "She doesn't live here anymore." I wouldn't have to say, "She's dead." But for gentiles, for those who lived out the war at home, such a bland statement—"She doesn't work here anymore"—could simply be the truth. Uncomplicated. Unburdened by what can't be said.

I could go to her house, as I once did. I could ring the bell this time instead of lurking on the sidewalk. But I'm tired. My back hurts. What would we possibly say?

On my way home, a woman stops on the sidewalk and glares at me.

"More of you came back than left," she says. "You all should have died."

Her hatred inflames me. How does she even know that I'm a survivor, a Jew? And what makes her speak to me in such a horrible way?

Yet part of me agrees with her. We all should have died. Then no one would be left to feel the constant, piercing loss.

Occasionally, our doorbell rings, and I jolt up in bed. These are the best moments. Someone is waiting outside the door, and in the seconds before we open it, that person could be anyone. Sometimes I imagine it is our father. He survived the first selection after all. He found a way to work, to appear young throughout the rest of the war, and here he is, smoking a cigarette, holding a piece of chalk, a long measuring tape slung around his neck like a scarf. Sometimes it is Eric I imagine on the stoop. He holds a bouquet of roses.

One day Lester Korda, one of the two brothers who rode with us on the train from Wels to Vienna, rings the bell. He has come to see how we are making out. "Call me Csicsi," he says. He is like fresh air rushing into our stale rooms. We are in an ongoing limbo, my sisters and me, between looking back and moving on. So much of our energy is used just to restore things—our health, our belongings, what we can of life before loss and imprisonment. Csicsi's warmth and interest in our welfare remind me that there is more to live for than that.

Klara is in the other room, practicing violin. Csicsi's eyes light up when he hears the music. "May I meet the musician?" he asks, and Klara obliges. She plays a Hungarian czardas. Csicsi dances. Maybe it is time to build our lives—not back to what they were, but anew.

Csicsi becomes a regular visitor. When Klara has to travel to Prague for another concert, Csicsi offers to go with her.

"Shall I bake a wedding cake now?" Magda asks.

"Stop it," Klara says. "He has a girlfriend. He's just being polite."

"Are you sure you're not falling in love?" I ask.

"He remembers our parents," she says, "and I remember his."

Another afternoon, when Magda and Klara are both away, a woman comes to our door. She has deep brown eyes. She asks for my father. She must be a customer, I think.

"He hasn't returned," I say, as though he's only gone to play billiards with his friends or to Paris to buy cloth.

Her eyes fill with tears.

"I loved him very much," she says.

The pieces click into place. She's not a former client come to see about a suit or a dress. She's his lover. His mistress. Part of me wants to hold tightly to her, this link to my father. I want to invite her inside, become her friend, listen to anything she can tell me about my father. Yet her existence also introduces me to a father who is a stranger. Who led a secret life. To let her memories of him into my sphere feels like betraying my own.

Before I can summon words, she hands me an envelope. "If he comes back," she says, "please give him this."

I close the door behind her, the letter in my hand like a trap. If I throw it away, it's like losing hope that he'll return someday. If I keep it, my sisters will ask what it is, who it's from. I used to prize those rare occasions when I knew something my sisters didn't. Now I feel punished by knowing.

I compromise. I tuck the letter in between two dusty books on a shelf.

The woman's visit convinces me that it's time to know about Eric. I walk to his house, barely strong enough, my heart pounding, my body combusting with too many feelings—excitement, fear, dread. He has kept me company these many awful months. He's kept me alive. But I am trading that fantasy now for whatever is real.

I force my feet to move. *It's temporary*, I tell myself. One step. Another step. Uncertainty has me in its jaws. But it won't last forever. It will transform into something else. Maybe passionate love. Maybe estrangement or disappointment. Maybe grief.

I arrive at the door. I'm shaking. My hand is lead. I steady myself against the brick before reaching for the bell. I ring it and wait, holding my breath. Blood rushes in my head, loud, pounding. I ring again, sweat cooling on my skin, my body suddenly cold despite the warm sun. I'm about to count my losses and walk away when the door opens a crack, then wider, a housekeeper standing in the entryway, eyeing me with curious suspicion.

I tell her my name. My voice squeaks. I tell her I'm looking for Eric. For a moment it seems she's about to ask me inside, to tell me to wait please while she calls for him.

"I'm sorry," she says. "I've been looking after the property for over a year. No one in the family has returned." I don't know what compels her to add one more word to the sentence, whether she says it to reassure herself or to comfort me. "*Yet*," she says. "No one has returned *yet*."

I am sobbing. She gives me a shy, sad smile, then closes the door, and I make my way home, barely able to see through the sheets of tears pouring down my face. Magda and Klara put me back in bed. They hold me, one on either side, while I weep.

"Dicuka, Dicuka," they say.

I cry because it seems I'll never sleep with my head on Eric's chest. I cry because the way my sisters hold me is love too.

"Shhh," my sisters say, rubbing my back, my head. They remind me that many survivors are still in displaced persons camps all over Europe. That we can scour the United Nations Relief and Rehabilitation Administration newspapers for familiar names among the list of survivors scattered over the Continent.

I weep for all I have and don't have.

Klara mothers me in earnest now. She does it out of love and a natural competence. I think she also does it out of guilt. She wasn't there to protect us at Auschwitz. She will protect us now. She does all the cooking. She feeds me with a spoon like I'm a baby. I love her, I love her attention, I love being held and made to feel safe. But it is suffocating too. Her kindness leaves me no breathing room. And she seems to need something from me in return. Not gratitude or appreciation. Something deeper. I can feel that she relies on me for her own sense of purpose. For her reason for being. In taking care of me, she finds the reason she was spared. My role is to be healthy enough to stay alive yet helpless enough to need her. That is my reason for having survived.

By the end of June, my back still isn't healed. There is a constant crunching, piercing feeling between my shoulder blades. And my chest still hurts, even to breathe. Then I break out in a fever. Klara takes me to the hospital. She insists that I be given a private room, the very best care. I worry about the expense, but she says she will just play more concerts; she will find a way to cover it. When the doctor comes in to examine me, I recognize him. He's the older brother of my former schoolmate. His name is Gaby. I remember that his sister called him the Angel Gabriel. She is dead now, I learn. She died at Auschwitz. He asks me if I ever saw her there. I wish I had a last image for him to remember her by, and I consider lying, telling him a story in which I witnessed her do something brave or heard her speak of him lovingly. But I don't lie. I would rather face the unknowns about my father and Eric than be told something that, however comforting, isn't true. The Angel Gabriel gives me my first medical attention since liberation. He diagnoses me with typhoid fever, pneumonia, pleurisy, and a broken back. He makes a removable cast for me that covers my whole torso. I place it on the bed at night so that I can climb inside it, my plaster shell.

Gaby visits the house to check on me. He doesn't charge me for his medical care. We sit and reminisce. Aside from the day I visited Eric's house and my sisters held me while I cried, I can't grieve with them, not explicitly. It's too raw, too present. And to grieve with them seems like a defilement of the miracle of our togetherness. But with Gaby I can speak and grieve more openly. One day I ask him about Eric. Gaby remembers him but doesn't know what became of him. Gaby has colleagues working at a repatriation center in the Tatra Mountains where some survivors of the camps stayed on their way home. He says he will ask them to see what they can learn about Eric.

One afternoon Gaby examines my back. He waits until I am lying down on my stomach to tell me what he has learned. "Eric was sent to Auschwitz," he says. "He died in January. The day before liberation."

I erupt in a wail. I think my chest will break. The blast of sorrow is so severe that tears won't come—only a jagged moaning in my throat. I am not yet capable of clear thoughts or questions about my beloved's last days, about his suffering, about the state of his mind and his spirit when his body gave out. I am consumed by the grief and injustice of losing him. If he could have held on for a few more hours, maybe even just a few more breaths, we could be together now. I moan into the table until my voice goes hoarse.

As the shock dissolves, I understand that, in a strange way, the pain of knowing is merciful. I have no such certainty about my own father's death. To know for sure that Eric is gone is like receiving a diagnosis after a long ache. I can pinpoint the reason for the hurt. I can clarify what has to heal.

But a diagnosis is not a cure. I don't know what to do with Eric's voice now, the remembered syllables, the hope.

Chapter 13
THE CHOICE

By the end of July my fever is gone, but Gaby still isn't satisfied with my progress. My lungs, compressed too long by my broken back, are full of fluid. He worries that I might have contracted tuberculosis and recommends that I go to a TB hospital in the Tatra Mountains, near the repatriation center where he learned of Eric's death. Klara will accompany me on the train to the nearest village in the mountains. Magda will stay at the apartment. After the effort of reclaiming it, on the off chance of an unexpected visitor, we can't risk leaving it empty, even for a day. Klara tends to me on the journey as if I am a child. "Look at my little one!" she exclaims to fellow passengers. I beam at them like a precocious toddler. I practically look like one. My hair has fallen out again from the typhoid and is just starting to grow back, baby soft. Klara helps me cover my head with a scarf. As we gain elevation, the dry alpine air feels clean in my chest, but it's still hard to breathe. There is a constant sludge in my lungs. It's as though all the tears I can't allow myself to shed on the outside are draining into a pool inside. I can't ignore the grief, but I can't seem to expel it either.

Klara is due back in Košice for another radio performance—her concerts are our only source of income—and can't accompany me to the TB hospital where I am to stay until I am well, but she refuses to let me go alone. We ask around at the repatriation center to see if anyone knows of someone going to the hospital, and I'm told that a young man staying in the nearby hotel is also going there to be treated. When I approach him in the lobby of the hotel, he is kissing a girl.

"Meet me at the train," he growls.

When I approach him on the train platform, he is still kissing the girl. He is dark haired, maybe ten years older than I am, though the war has made it harder to tell a person's age. I will turn eighteen in September, but with my skinny limbs and flat chest and bald head, I look more like twelve. I stand beside them awkwardly as they embrace, not sure how to get his attention. I'm annoyed. *This* is the man to whom I'm to be entrusted?

"Could you help me, sir?" I finally ask. "You are supposed to escort me to the hospital."

"I'm busy," he says. He barely breaks his kiss to respond to me. He is like an older sibling shaking away an annoying sister. "Meet me on the train."

After Klara's constant fawning and attention, his dismissiveness cuts. I don't know why it bothers me so much. Is it that his girlfriend is alive while my boyfriend is dead? Or is it that I am already so diminished that without another person's attention or approval, I feel I am in danger of disappearing entirely?

He buys me a sandwich on the train and a newspaper for himself. We don't talk, other than to exchange names and formalities. Béla is his name. To me he is just a rude person on a train, a person I must grudgingly ask for help, a person who only grudgingly gives it.

When we arrive at the station, we learn we have to walk to the TB hospital, and now there is no newspaper to distract him.

"What did you do before the war?" he asks. I notice what I didn't hear before—he speaks with a stutter. When I tell him that I was a gymnast and I danced ballet, he says, "That reminds me of a joke."

I look at him expectantly, ready for a dose of Hungarian humor, ready for the relief I felt at Auschwitz when Magda and I hosted the boob contest with our bunkmates, the lift of laughter in terrible times.

"There was a bird," he says, "and the bird was about to die. A cow came and warmed him up a little—from her rear end, if you know what I mean—and the bird started to perk up. Then a truck came and finished off the bird. A wise old horse came by and saw the dead bird on the road. The horse said, 'Didn't I tell you if you have shit on your head, don't dance?'" Béla laughs at his own joke.

But I feel insulted. He means to be funny, but I think he is trying to tell me, you have shit on your head. I think he means, you're a real mess. I think he's saying, you shouldn't call yourself a dancer if you look like this. For a moment, before his insult, it had been such a relief to have his attention, such a relief to be asked who I was before the war. Such a relief to acknowledge the me who existed—who thrived—before the war. His joke reinforces how irreparably the war has changed and damaged me. It hurts for a stranger to cut me down. It hurts because he's right. I am a mess. Still, I won't let an insensitive man or his Hungarian sarcasm get the last word. I will show him that the buoyant dancer still lives in me, no matter how short my hair is, how thin my face, how thick the grief in my chest. I bound ahead of him and do the splits in the middle of the road.

I don't have TB, as it turns out. They keep me for three weeks in the hospital all the same to treat the fluid building up in my lungs. I am so afraid of contracting TB that I open doors with my feet instead of my hands, even though I know the disease can't be spread through touch, or through germs on doorknobs. It is a good thing that I don't have TB, but I am still not well. I don't have the vocabulary to explain the flooded feeling in my chest, the dark throb in my forehead. It's like grit smeared across my vision. It takes effort to get out of bed. There's the effort of breath. And, worse, the existential effort. Why get up? What is there to get up for? I wasn't suicidal at Auschwitz. I never considered hanging myself or throwing myself at the fence. I kept hope alive. *If I survive today, tomorrow I will be free.*

The irony of freedom is that it is harder to find hope and purpose. In the death camps, when I spent each and every day surrounded by people who said, "The only way you'll get out of here is as a corpse," the dire prophecies gave me something to fight against. Now the only demons are within. The anger boiling over in my belly about the life that was stolen from me. It isn't just the irrevocable loss that hurts. It's the way it ripples out into the future. The way it perpetuates. My mother used to tell me to look for a man with a wide forehead because that means he's intelligent. "Watch how he uses his handkerchief," she would say. "Make sure he always carries a clean one. Make sure his shoes are polished." She won't be at my wedding. She won't ever know who I become, whom I choose. Why not choose not to be?

Every day from now on will have pain in it. Grief doesn't happen once. It lasts forever. It happens for the rest of your life. What is the point, what is the point, what is the point?

Béla has been assigned the room right above mine. One day he stops by my room to check on me.

"I'll make you laugh," he says, "and that will make you better. You'll see."

He waggles his tongue, pulls on his ears, makes animal noises, the way you might entertain a baby. It's absurd, maybe insulting, yet I can't help myself. The laugh rises out of me like a tide. "Don't laugh," the doctors had warned me, as though laughter were a constant temptation, as though I were in danger of laughing to death. "If you laugh, you will have more pain." They were right. It does hurt, but it also feels good.

I lie awake that night thinking of him in the room just above mine, thinking up things to impress him, things I studied in school.

The next day, when he visits my room, I tell him everything I have been able to remember in the night about Greek myths, calling up the most obscure gods and goddesses. I tell him about Freud's *Interpretation of Dreams.* I perform for him, the way I used to perform for my parents' dinner guests, my turn in the spotlight before Klara, the headlining act, took the stage. He looks at me the way a teacher looks at a star pupil. He tells me very little about himself, but I do learn that he studied violin when he was young and still loved to play chamber music recordings and conduct in the air.

Béla is twenty-seven years old. I am only a child. He has other women in his life. The woman he was kissing on the train platform when I interrupted him. And, he tells me, another patient here at the TB hospital, his cousin Marianna's best friend, a girl he dated in high school, before the war. She is very ill. She isn't going to make it. He calls himself her fiancé, a gesture of hope for her on her deathbed, a gesture of hope for her mother. There's also a wife—a near stranger, a woman with whom he was never intimate, a gentile with whom he made an arrangement on paper in the early days of the war in an effort to protect his family and his fortune.

It isn't love. It's that I am hungry, so very hungry, and I amuse him. And he looks at me the way Eric did that long-ago day in the book club, as though I am intelligent, as though I have worthwhile things to say. For now, that's enough.

On my last night at the TB hospital, the girl in the bed next to mine gestures for me to come sit beside her. She's very ill, too weak to talk, but she smiles softly at me and places a gift in my hands—a beautiful pleated skirt. I understand why she's giving it to me. She knows she isn't going home, that she will live whatever days or weeks or months she has left right here in this bed. She doesn't have a choice. But I do.

I climb into bed. I lie in the dark, feeling the cool of the sheets, the snugness of the room. I think of the dying girl beside me and how she could have treated me with jealousy or turned her face to the wall. Even a girl with a death sentence has choices. And I have them too. A voice comes to me, from the bottom of the mountains, from the very center of the Earth. Up through the floor and thin mattress, it envelops me, charges me. *If you live*, the voice says, *you've got to stand for something.*

"I'll write to you," Béla says in the morning when we say goodbye. It's not love. I don't hold him to it.

Yet something in me has shifted. I don't hear the endless drone in my head of "Why me?" and "What's the point?" The tune of despair, pointlessness, and victimhood has changed. "What's next?" I hear myself singing. I'm curious. I'm alive. I'm here. I'm still weak and healing, but I feel that I can face whatever comes to me. That anything that happens opens a door, creates an opportunity to find out, What now? What now? Which direction will I go next? Which arrow will I follow?

When I arrive in Košice, Magda meets me at the train station. Klara has been so possessive of me since our reunion that I have forgotten what it is like to be alone with Magda. Her hair has grown. Waves frame her face. Her eyes are bright again. She looks well.

She is bursting with gossip from the three weeks that I've been away. Csicsi has broken things off with his girlfriend and is now unabashedly courting Klara. The Košice survivors have formed an entertainment club, and she has already promised that I will perform. And Laci, the man from the top of the train, has written to tell us that he has received an affidavit of support from his relatives in Texas. Soon he will join them in a place called El Paso, she tells me, where he will work in their furniture store and save money for medical school.

"Klara better not humiliate me by marrying first," Magda says.

This is how we will heal. Yesterday, cannibalism and murder. Yesterday, choosing blades of grass. Today, the antiquated customs and proprieties, the rules and roles that make us feel normal.

"Here," my sister says. "I have something for you." She hands me an envelope, my name written on it in the cursive script we were taught to write in school. "Your old friend came by."

For a moment I think she means Eric. He is alive. Inside the envelope is my future. He has waited for me. Or he has already moved on.

But the envelope isn't from Eric. And it doesn't contain my future. It holds my past. It holds a picture of me, perhaps the last picture taken of me before Auschwitz, the picture Eric took of me doing the splits, the picture I gave to my friend for safekeeping. In my fingers I hold the me who has yet to lose her parents, who doesn't know how soon she will lose her love.

Magda takes me to the entertainment club gathering that night. Klara and Csicsi are there, and Csicsi's brother Imre, and my old friend Sara, who also survived. Gaby, my doctor, is there too, and perhaps that is why, weak as I am, I agree to dance. I want to show him I am getting well. I want to show him that the time he has devoted to my care has made a difference, that he hasn't wasted his effort. I ask Klara and the other musicians to play "The Blue Danube," and I begin my routine, the same dance that a little more than a year ago I performed my first night at Auschwitz, the dance that Josef Mengele rewarded with a loaf of bread. The steps have not changed, but my body has. I have none of the lean, limber muscle, none of the strength in my limbs or my core. I am a wheezing husk, a broken-backed girl with no hair. I close my eyes as I did in the barracks. That long-ago night I held my lids shut so that I wouldn't have to look at Mengele's terrifying and murderous eyes, so that I could keep from crumpling to the ground under the force of his stare. Now I close my eyes so that I can feel my body, not escape the room, so that I can feel the heat of appreciation from my audience. As I find my way back to the movements, to the familiar steps, the high kick, the splits, I grow more confident and comfortable in the moment. And I find my way back in time, to the days when we could imagine no worse encroachment on our freedom than curfews or yellow stars. I dance toward my innocence. Toward the girl who bounded up the stairs to the ballet studio. Toward the wise and loving mother who first brought her there. *Help me*, I call to her. *Help me. Help me to live again.*

A few days later, a thick letter arrives, addressed to me. It's from Béla. It is the first of many long letters he will write, first from the TB hospital and then from his home in Prešov, where he was born and raised—the third-largest city in Slovakia, just twenty miles north of Košice. As I learn more about Béla and begin to assemble the facts he gives me in these letters into a life, the man with a stutter and sarcastic sense of humor becomes a person with contours.

Béla's earliest memory, he writes, is of going for a walk with his grandfather, one of the wealthiest men in the country, and being denied a cookie from the patisserie. When he leaves the hospital, he will take over this same grandfather's business, wholesaling produce from the region's farmers, grinding coffee and grinding wheat for all of Slovakia. Béla is a full pantry, a country of plenty. He is a feast.

Like my mother, Béla lost one of his parents when he was very young. His father, who had been the mayor of Prešov, and before that, a renowned lawyer for the poor, went to a conference in Prague the winter Béla was four. He stepped off the train and fell into an avalanche of snow, where he suffocated. Or that is what the police told Béla's mother. Béla suspects that his father—a controversial figure who offended the Prešov elite by serving as an advocate for the poor and disenfranchised—was murdered. Ever since his father's death, Béla has spoken with a stutter.

His mother never recovered from his father's death. Her father-in-law, Béla's grandfather, kept her locked up in the house to keep her from meeting other men. During the war, Béla's aunt and uncle invited her to join them in Hungary, where they were living in hiding using false identification papers. One day Béla's mother was at the market when she saw a group of SS soldiers. She panicked. She ran up to them and shouted a confession. "I am Jewish!" she said. They shipped her off to Auschwitz, where she died in the gas chamber. The rest of the family, exposed by Béla's mother's confession, managed to flee to the mountains.

Béla's brother, George, has lived in America since before the war. Before he immigrated, he was walking down the street in Bratislava, the capital of Slovakia, when he was attacked by gentiles, his glasses broken. He left the brewing anti-Semitism in Europe to live with their great-uncle in Chicago. Their cousin Marianna escaped to England. Béla, though he had studied in England as a boy and spoke English fluently, refused to leave Slovakia. He wanted to protect everyone in his family. That was not to be. His grandfather died of stomach cancer. And his aunt and uncle, coaxed out of the mountains by Germans who promised that all Jews who returned would be treated kindly, were lined up in the street and shot.

Béla escaped the Nazis by hiding in the mountains. He could barely hold a screwdriver, he writes. He was afraid of weapons, he didn't want to fight, he was clumsy, but he became a partisan. He took up a gun and joined ranks with the Russians who were fighting the Nazis. While with the partisans, he contracted TB. He hadn't had to survive the camps. Instead, he had survived the mountain forests. For this I am grateful. I will never see the imprint of the smokestacks mirrored in his eyes.

Prešov is only an hour's drive from Košice. One weekend Béla visits me, pulling Swiss cheese and salami from a bag. Food. If I can keep him interested in me, he will feed me and my sisters—this is what I think. I don't pine for him the way I did for Eric. I don't fantasize about kissing him or long to have him near. I don't even flirt—not in a romantic way. We are like two shipwrecked people staring at the sea for signs of life. And in each other we see a glimmer.

My friend Sara is another glimmer. She visits me one afternoon and tells me she has met someone. They're planning to get married.

"Already?" I ask. "Why the rush?" I think I am protecting her from deciding out of duress, from choosing something in dire times that she might later regret. But maybe what I really mean is "Don't leave me behind."

"Edith," she says, "we're going on eighteen. And after what we've been through—our childhoods ended a long time ago. I don't want to sit around suffering. I want to move on."

She tells me that she and her husband will build their new life in Palestine.

A lump forms in my throat in exactly the spot where I learned to taste hope in Auschwitz. But those dreams I held close are truly impossible now. Eric is dead. I don't want to spoil Sara's happy news, but the tears come fast and hard. I can't press them down.

Sara holds my hand. "I wish we could bring them back," she says. She means Eric, and our parents, and our classmates, and six million mothers, fathers, sisters, brothers, professors, doctors, musicians, bricklayers, tailors, shopkeepers, factory workers, students, babies.

"Eric and I should have left," I say. "He wanted to go to Palestine. I should have said yes. If I'd said yes, he would still be alive."

Sara strokes my hand. "We didn't know," she says. "You did the best with what you had."

Regret sloshes in my gut and chest like poison. "I should have known," I say. It's easier to punish myself than accept the grief. If it's my fault, then I can keep living forever in a world where I could have made a different choice instead of the world where Eric is gone.

"You could still go to Palestine," Sara says. "You could come with me. You could live there in honor of Eric. And"—she shines her kind smile on me—"you could fall in love again. Isn't that the best way to celebrate that we're alive?"

Sara's words are in my mind when Béla visits again, as I watch him pull more rich cheeses and meats from his bag. I find that I am happy to see him. This contentment has to do with the food, but it also has to do with the jokes he tells, with the growing sense of belonging I feel in his presence. Maybe love has different flavors and textures. No one can ever replace Eric. He will always be my first love, the love that helped me survive. Maybe that love never goes away. It existed all those months in a death camp. Maybe love transcends not only physical absence but also death. *The spirit never dies*, Magda said that first day at Auschwitz as we mourned our mother's death. Maybe Eric is still with me now in some way. Maybe he's laughing at my shaggy hair, my hunger for Swiss cheese, my growing affection for an older man with a stutter.

When Béla leaves that evening to drive home, I walk him to his car.

"Editke," he murmurs in my ear as he hugs me. His hands linger on my waist.

A warmth gathers in me. I lift my face. His kiss tastes like salt and cream. I don't know how much of my heart I can give to him. Yet if I allow it, I know I can be nourished here.

When I tell my sisters that I've started a relationship with Béla, Magda says, "Big surprise." Flirting is her game. Here I am usurping her tool.

Klara's words cut worse. She turns to Magda and says, "Ah, two cripples hooking up. How's that going to work?"

Later, at the table, she speaks to me directly. "You're a baby, Dicuka," she says. "You can't make decisions like this. You're not whole. And he isn't either. He has TB. He stutters. You can't be with him."

Now I have a new motivation for this relationship to work. I have to prove my sister wrong.

Klara's objection isn't the only impediment to being with Béla. There is also the fact that he is still legally married to the gentile woman who protected his family fortune from the Nazis, and she refuses to divorce him. They have never lived together, never had a relationship of any kind other than that of convenience—for her, his money;

for him, her gentile status—but she won't grant him the divorce, not at first, not until he agrees to pay her a large sum of money.

And then there is his fiancée in the Tatra Mountains, dying of TB. He begs her friend Marianna, his cousin who had escaped to England but returned after the war, to deliver the news that he isn't going to marry her. Marianna is justifiably furious. "You're horrible!" she yells. "You can't do this to her. I won't in a million years tell her you're breaking your promise."

Béla asks me to come with him back to the hospital so he can tell her himself. We take the same train we rode months earlier when he buried himself in a newspaper.

"I guess you learned to like the bird with shit on her head," I say.

Béla chuckles. I feel that warmth run through me, that feeling that could be love.

The fiancée is gracious and kind to me, and very, very ill. I know I must be healing now because it rattles me to see someone so physically devastated. It is too much like the recent past. I am afraid to stand so close to death's door. She tells me she is happy that Béla has found someone like me, someone with so much energy and life. I am glad to have her blessing. And yet how easily I could have been the one in bed, propped up on scratchy pillows, coughing between words, filling a handkerchief with blood.

That night Béla and I stay in a hotel together, the hotel where we met when Klara asked him to chaperone me to the hospital. For the first time, we will share a room and share a bed. I try to remember the forbidden words in Zola's *Nana*, and what my married bunkmate at Auschwitz told me, and anything else that can prepare me for the dance of intimacy.

We sit on the edge of the bed, fully clothed. Part of me wants to flee the room; part of me wants to tear off my clothes. To finally do and feel the things I've only imagined.

"You're shivering," Béla says. "Are you cold?" He goes to his suitcase and takes out a package wrapped with a shining bow.

Inside the box, nestled in tissue paper, is a beautiful silk negligee. It is an extravagant gift. But that isn't what moves me. He somehow knew that I would need a second skin. It isn't that I want to shield myself from him, to cover my nakedness. It's that I need a way to heighten myself, extend, a way to step into the chapter that hasn't been written yet. I go to the bathroom to change, and I tremble as I slip the garment over my head, as the fabric falls against my legs. The right costume can augment the dance. I step back into the room and twirl for him.

"*Izléses*," he says. Classy.

His gaze is more than a compliment. In his eyes I find a new appreciation of my body—of my life.

When we return to Košice, Béla says he wants to take me dancing.

"This will be a real date," he says. "We'll eat at a restaurant."

As I get ready, I think of Eric's invitation for our first date, the white skirt I wore, the American jazz. I'm a different person now. I put on the pleated skirt, the gift from the dying girl at the TB hospital. I'll dance because she can't.

At the restaurant I feel myself stiffening. Sometimes my body still feels like a doll with stuck joints, a doll that I try fruitlessly to move around. Sometimes living feels like pretending. I feel confused by the menu. It was awful to starve, yet the daily ladle of soup was consistent, a known thing in a place where everything else was shocking and uncertain. Now I feel overwhelmed by choices. I feel guilty receiving these offerings.

Béla senses my distress and orders for me. "While we wait for the food," he says, "let's dance."

He pulls me to my feet and leads me to the dance floor. I think of the GI in Wels. Of my ballet teacher, lifting me over his head. *All your ecstasy in life will come from the inside.* I give myself to Béla's arms, to the music, to my body, now fluid and strong. Béla is a beautiful dancer. I don't know why I'm being given this gift, but my mind quiets. I stop teething on the question of what I deserve.

Béla spins me and dips me, smiling down. "Girl, you can dance," he says.

As we walk back to our table to eat our meal, a man waves to me and motions us over.

"I'm Gyorgy," he says. "I knew your boyfriend, Eric. I met you once or twice. Before the war."

Gyorgy invites us to sit. "You know Eric died?" he asks.

I nod. "I heard it was just before the camp was liberated."

"Yes." Gyorgy's voice is solemn. Quiet. "I was with him in the camp."

I sit in the silence. He's opened a door. I can ask for more information. I can ask if Eric spoke of me, if he loved me till the end. I can ask how sick he was, if he had any last words. I can ask for details, for new lines with which to paint my grief. Yet if I ask, then I know. Then I have to see Eric not just as a person who is gone but as a person who suffered and died.

"I'm not sure I should tell you this," Gyorgy says, "but I think you should know."

My chest tightens. Béla squeezes my hand.

"You can tell me," I say.

Gyorgy takes a deep breath. "You know how idealistic Eric was," he says.

The word "was" makes me tremble. Using the past tense to describe Eric feels untrue. I resist it. But I nod, thinking of Eric's passionate views on Palestine and his ambition to practice medicine.

"He was mentally and physically strong," Gyorgy continues, "but the camp was very hard on his spirit. It was hard for him to accept that humans could annihilate other humans so systematically."

"No one should accept that," Béla interjects.

"No," Gyorgy agrees. "But Eric lost his will to continue living in such a world."

I am hardly breathing. My throat is dry. I feel that if I breathe, I'll choke.

"He—" Gyorgy breaks off, as though reassessing his decision to speak the truth.

I sit, rigid in the ominous silence. I wait for what I must hear.

"At first I saw him withdrawing. I thought it was hunger.

Fatigue. Cold. But then I noticed that he would barely touch his evening soup. One January day, he ran into the barbed wires. He took his life."

My mind feels upended, churning, frozen. Eric, his bright eyes, his fresh-grass smell, the last words he said to me, *I'll never forget your eyes. I'll never forget your hands.* He was so full of life and vim and determination. I believed he could be crushed by cruelty but not that he would give up.

"I shouldn't have told you," Gyorgy says. He stares at the table. "I'm sorry."

"It's okay," I say. "I'd rather know. It's not who I knew him to be. It's hard to picture him resigning."

"If it helps," Gyorgy says, "I've come to see it differently. Not that he gave up. That he wanted to be in charge of his own death."

Does he regret it now? I wonder. If he'd stayed just one more day, he would be alive. He would be free. He would be here dancing with me.

"Let the food get cold," I tell Béla as we leave Gyorgy's table. "I need to dance."

He smiles at me, this man who may soon be my husband, this man who might become the father of my children, this man with whom I am alive, right now, in a room full of music. Béla takes my hand in his, puts his other hand at the small of my back. As we begin to move, it strikes me that maybe, somehow, Eric has brought Béla to me. That Eric is our matchmaker. Béla spins us, steady and fast, through the warm room, and my mind leaps with questions. Where will we build our life? What will we do with the life we've been given? While uncertainty was part of the torture and horror of Auschwitz, forcing us to wonder every day if this would be our last, it also made me curious. My hope saved me in the death camps, and so did my hunger to know, *What will happen next?*

I dance, I dance, my head against his chest.

Epilogue
LEAVE A STONE

Almost forty years later, I wake in a hotel room in Germany, Béla fast asleep beside me. We've shared many dances by now and many struggles. We fled oppressive Communist rule in Europe, losing everything we owned to become immigrants in America, working in factories for pennies, learning English by reading the picture books our daughter brought home from preschool. We went back to school, building careers, Béla as an accountant and me as a psychologist. We've raised three children and become grandparents—our best revenge on Hitler, Béla says. We've come to find in each other a deep and steady love—not the butterflies and tingles of smitten romance, but the act of showing up every day, of choosing each other again and again. His love is a harbor, a place where I seek shelter. And it's a studio where I practice and grow and limber up, where I learn and relearn my strength.

Béla stirs and opens his eyes. He smiles at me, his face all gentleness and twinkle.

"I'm ready," I tell him. It's my first time in Germany since the war—a trip I was terrified to make. But there's something else I need to do before we go home. A rite of grief, of coming to terms. A rite of self-acceptance. "I'm ready to go back to Auschwitz."

"Please come back with me," I beg Magda on the phone later that morning.

I can't imagine returning to hell without my sister. I wouldn't have survived without her. I can't survive going back to our prison now unless she is beside me, holding my hand. I know it's not possible to relive the past, to be who I used to be, to hug my mother again, even once. There is nothing that can alter the past, that can make me different from who I am, change what was done to my parents, done to Eric, done to me. There is no going back. I know this. But I can't ignore the feeling that there is something waiting for me in my old prison, something to recover. Or discover. Some long-lost part of me.

"What kind of a crazy masochist do you think I am?" Magda says. "Why the hell would I go back there? Why would you?"

It's a fair question. Am I only punishing myself? Reopening a wound? Maybe I will regret it. But I think I will regret it more if I don't go back.

No matter how many ways I try to convince her, Magda refuses. Magda is choosing never to return, and I respect her for it. But I will make a different choice.

Béla and I travel to Salzburg, where we tour the cathedral constructed on the ruins of a Roman church. It has been rebuilt three times, we learn—most recently after a bomb damaged the central dome during the war. There is no evidence of the destruction.

"Like us," Béla says, taking my hand.

From Salzburg, we go to Vienna, traveling over the same ground Magda and I marched across before we were liberated. I see ditches running alongside roads, and I imagine them as I once saw them, spilling over with corpses, but I can also see them as they are now, filling up with summer grass. I can see that the past doesn't taint the present, and the present doesn't diminish the past. Time is the medium. Time is the track; we travel it. The train goes through Linz. Through Wels. I am a girl with a broken back who learns to write a capital *G* again, who learns again to dance.

We spend the night in Vienna, not far from the Rothschild Hospital, where we once lived many years ago when we were waiting for our visas to America. In the morning we board another train north, heading for Copenhagen to visit friends.

I think Béla assumes my desire to return to Auschwitz might wane, but on our second morning in Copenhagen I ask our friends for directions to the Polish embassy. They caution me about their survivor friends who visited the camp and then died. "Don't retraumatize yourself," they plead.

Béla, too, looks worried. "Hitler didn't win," I remind him.

I thought that choosing to return would be the biggest hurdle. But at the Polish embassy, Béla and I learn that labor riots have broken out across Poland, that the Soviets might intervene to suppress the demonstrations, that the embassy has been advised to stop issuing travel visas to Westerners. Béla is ready to console me, but I brush him away. I feel my force of will expand. I have come this far in my life and my healing. I can concede to no obstacle now.

"I'm a survivor," I tell the embassy clerk. "I was a prisoner at Auschwitz. My parents and grandparents died there. I fought so hard to survive. Please don't make me wait to go back." I don't know that within a year Polish-American relations will have deteriorated, that they will stay frozen for the rest of the decade, that this is in fact the last chance for me and Béla to go to Auschwitz together. I only know that I can't let myself be turned back.

The clerk eyes me, expressionless. He steps away from the counter, returns. "Passports," he says. Into our blue American passports, he has inserted travel visas good for one week. "Enjoy Poland," he says.

This is when I start to feel afraid. On the train to Kraków, I feel that I'm in a crucible, that I am reaching the point at which I will break or burn, that fear alone could turn me into ash. *This is here. This is now.* I try to reason with the part of me that feels that with every mile I travel I lose a layer of skin. I will be a skeleton again by the time I get to Poland. I want to be more than bones.

"Let's get off at the next stop," I tell Béla. "It's not important to go all the way to Auschwitz. Let's go home."

"Edie," he says, "you're going to be fine. It's only a place. It can't hurt you."

I stay on the train for another stop, and another, through

Berlin, through Poznań. I think of Dr. Hans Selye—a fellow Hungarian—who said stress is the body's response to any demand for change. Our automatic responses are to fight or to flee—but in Auschwitz, where we endured more than stress, where we lived in *dis*tress, the stakes life and death, never knowing what would happen next, the options to fight or flee didn't exist. I would have been shot if I'd fought back, electrocuted if I'd tried to run away. So I learned to flow, to dance instead of fight. I learned to stay in the situation, to develop the only thing I had left, to look within for the part of me that no Nazi could ever murder. To find and hold on to my truest self. Maybe I'm not losing skin. Maybe I am only stretching. Stretching to encompass every aspect of who I am—and have been—and can become.

It is the middle of the afternoon when we reach Kraków. We will sleep here tonight—or try to. Tomorrow we will take a cab to Auschwitz. Béla wants to tour the Old Town, and I try to pay attention to the medieval architecture, but my mind is too heavy with expectation—a strange mix of promise and dread. We pause outside St. Mary's Basilica to hear the trumpeter play the *hejnał* that marks the top of every hour. A group of teenage boys jostles past us, joking loudly in Polish, but I don't feel their merriment, I feel anxious. These young men remind me how soon the next generation will come of age. Has my generation taught the youth well enough to prevent another Holocaust from occurring? Or will our hard-won freedom capsize in a new sea of hate?

I have had many opportunities to influence young people—my

own children and grandchildren, my former students, the audiences I address around the world, and individual patients. On the eve of my return to Auschwitz, my responsibility to them feels especially potent. It isn't just for myself that I'm going back. It's for all that ripples out from me.

Do I have what it takes to make a difference? Can I pass on my strength instead of my loss? My love instead of my hatred? I think of Corrie ten Boom, one of the Righteous Gentiles. She and her family resisted Hitler by hiding hundreds of Jews in their home, and she ended up in a concentration camp herself. Her sister perished there—she died in Corrie's arms. Corrie was released due to a clerical error one day before all of the inmates at Ravensbrück were executed. And a few years after the war, she met one of the most vicious guards at her camp, one of the men who were responsible for her sister's death. She could have spit on him, wished him death, cursed his name. But she prayed for the strength to forgive him, and she took his hands in her own. She says that in that moment, the former prisoner clasping the hands of the former guard, she felt the purest and most profound love.

Now, on the eve of my return to prison, I remind myself that each of us has an Adolf Hitler and a Corrie ten Boom within us. We have the capacity to hate and the capacity to love. Which one we reach for—our inner Hitler or our inner ten Boom—is up to us.

In the morning, we hire a cab to drive us the hour to Auschwitz. Béla engages the driver in chitchat about his family, his children. I take in the view I didn't see when I was sixteen, when I approached

Auschwitz from within the darkness of a cattle car. Farms, villages, green. Life continues, as it did all around us when we were imprisoned there.

The driver drops us off, and Béla and I are alone again, standing before my former prison. The wrought iron sign looms: ARBEIT MACHT FREI, work will set you free. My legs shake at the sight, at the memory of how these words gave my father hope. We will work until the end of the war, he thought. It will last for just a little while, and then we'll be free. *Arbeit Macht Frei.* These words kept us calm until the gas chamber doors locked around our loved ones, until panic was futile. And then these words became a daily, an hourly irony, because here nothing could set you free. Death was the only escape. And so even the idea of freedom became another form of hopelessness.

The grass is lush. The trees have filled in. But the clouds are the color of bone, and beneath them the man-made structures, even the ones in ruins, dominate the landscape. Miles and miles of relentless fence. A vast expanse of crumbling brick barracks and bare rectangular patches where buildings used to stand. The bleak horizontal lines—of barracks, fence, tower—are regular and orderly, but there is no life in this geometry. This is the geometry of systematic torture and death. Mathematical annihilation. And then I notice it again, the thing that haunted me those hellish months when this was my home: I can't see or hear a single bird. No birds live here. Not even now. The sky is bare of their wings, the silence deeper because of the absence of their song.

Tourists gather. Our tour commences. We are a small group

of eight or ten. The immensity crushes. I sense it in our stillness, in the way we almost stop breathing. There is no fathoming the enormity of the horror committed in this place. I was here while the fires burned. I woke and worked and slept to the stench of burning corpses, and even I can't fathom it. The brain tries to contain the numbers, tries to take in the confounding accumulation of things that have been assembled and put on display for the visitors—the suitcases wrested from the soon-to-be dead, the bowls and plates and cups, the thousands upon thousands of pairs of glasses amassed in a tangle like a surreal tumbleweed. The baby clothes crocheted by loving hands for babies who never became children or women or men. The sixty-seven-foot-long glass case filled entirely with human hair. We count: 4,700 corpses cremated in each fire, 75,000 Polish dead, 21,000 Gypsies, 15,000 Soviets.

The numbers accrue and accrue. We can form the equation—we can do the math that describes the more than one million dead at Auschwitz. We can add that number to the rosters of the dead at the thousands of other death camps in the Europe of my youth, to the corpses dumped in ditches or rivers before they were ever sent to a death camp. But there is no equation that can adequately summarize the effect of such total loss. There is no language that can explain the systematic inhumanity of this human-made death factory. More than one million people were murdered right here where I stand. It is the world's biggest cemetery. And in all the tens, hundreds, thousands, millions of dead, in all the possessions packed and then forcibly relinquished, in all the miles of fence and brick, another number looms. The number zero. Here in the world's biggest cemetery, there is not one single grave. Only the empty spaces where the crematories and gas chambers, hastily destroyed by the Nazis before liberation, stood. The bare patches of ground where my parents died.

We complete the tour of the men's camp. I still must go to the women's side, to Birkenau. That is why I am here. Béla asks if I want him to come with me, but I shake my head. This last piece of the journey I must travel alone.

I leave Béla at the entrance gate, and I am back in the past. Music plays through the loudspeakers, festive sounds that contradict the bleak surroundings. *You see*, my father says, *it can't be a terrible place. We'll only work a little, till the war's over.* It is temporary. We can survive this. He joins his line and waves to me. Do I wave back to him? O memory, tell me that I waved to my father before he died.

My mother links her arm in mine. We walk side by side. "Button your coat," she says. "Stand tall." I am back inside the image that has occupied my inward gaze for most of my life: three hungry women in wool coats, arms linked, in a barren yard. My mother. My sister. Me.

I am wearing the coat that I put on that April dawn, I am slim and athletic, my hair tucked back under a scarf. My mother scolds me again to stand tall. "You're a woman, not a child," she says. There is a purpose to her nagging. She wants me to look every day of my sixteen years and more. My survival depends on it.

And yet I won't for the life of me let go of my mother's hand. The guards point and shove. We inch forward in our line. I see

Mengele's heavy eyes ahead, the gapped teeth when he grins. He is conducting. He is an eager host. "Is anyone sick?" he asks, solicitous. "Over forty? Under fourteen? Go left, go left."

This is our last chance. To share words, to share silence. To embrace. This time I know it is the end. And still I come up short. I just want my mother to look at me. To reassure me. To look at me and never look away. What is this need I hand to her again and again, this impossible thing I want?

It's our turn now. Dr. Mengele lifts his finger. "Is she your mother or your sister?" he asks.

I cling to my mother's hand. Magda hugs her other side. I don't think about which word will protect her. I don't think at all. I only feel every single cell in me that loves her, that needs her. She is my mother, my mama, my only mama. And so I say the word that I have spent the rest of my life trying to banish from my consciousness, the word that I will always regret.

"Mother," I say.

As soon as the word is out of my mouth, I want to pull it back into my throat. I have realized too late the significance of the question. *Is she your mother or your sister?* "Sister, sister, sister!" I want to scream. Mengele points my mother to the left. She follows behind the young children and the elderly, the mothers who are pregnant or holding babies in their arms. I will follow her. I won't let her out of my sight. I begin to run toward my mother, but Mengele grabs my shoulder. "You'll see your mother very soon," he says. He pushes me to the right. Toward Magda. To the other side. To life.

"Mama!" I call. We are separated again, in memory as we were in life, but I will not let memory be another dead end. "Mama!" I say. I will not be satisfied with the back of her head. I must see the full sun of her face.

She turns to look at me. She is a point of stillness in the marching river of the other condemned. I feel her radiance, the beauty that was more than beauty, which she often hid under her sadness and disapproval. She sees me watching her. She smiles. It's a small smile. A sad smile.

"I should have said 'sister'! Why didn't I say 'sister'?" I call to her across the years, to ask her forgiveness. That is what I have returned to Auschwitz to receive, I think. To hear her tell me I did the best with what I knew. That I made the right choice.

But she can't say that, or even if she did, I wouldn't believe it. I can forgive the Nazis, but how can I forgive myself? I would live it all again, every selection line, every shower, every freezing-cold night and deadly roll call, every haunted meal, every breath of smoke-charred air, every time I nearly died or wanted to, if I could only live this moment over, this moment and the one just before it, when I could have made a different choice. When I could have given a different answer to Mengele's question. When I could have saved, if even for a day, my mother's life.

My mother turns away. I watch her gray coat, her soft shoulders, her hair that is coiled and shining, receding from me. I see her walk away with the other women and children, toward the locker rooms, where they will undress, where she will take off the coat that still holds Klara's caul, where they will be told to memorize the hook number where they've stored their clothes, as though they will be returning to that dress, to that coat, to that pair of shoes. My mother will stand naked with the other mothers—the grandmothers, the young mothers with their babies in their arms—and with the children of mothers who were sent to the line that Magda and I joined. She will file down the stairs into the room with showerheads on the walls, where more and more people will be pushed inside until the room is damp with sweat and tears and echoing with the cries of the terrified women and children, until it is packed and there is not enough air to breathe. Will she notice the small square windows in the ceiling through which the guards will push the poison? For how long will she know she is dying? Long enough to think of me and Magda and Klara? Of my father? Long enough to say a prayer to her mother? Long enough to feel angry at me for saying the word that in one quick second sent her to her death?

Could I have saved my mother? Maybe. And I will live for all of the rest of my life with that possibility. And I can castigate myself for having made the wrong choice. Or I can accept that the more important choice is *not* the one I made when I was hungry and terrified, when we were surrounded by dogs and guns and uncertainty, when I was sixteen; it's the one I make now. The choice to accept myself as I am: human, imperfect. And the choice to be responsible for my own happiness. To forgive my flaws and reclaim my innocence. To stop asking why I deserved to survive. To function as well as I can, to commit myself to serve others, to do everything in my power to honor my parents, to see to it that they did not die in vain. To do my best, in my limited capacity, so future generations don't experience what I did. To be useful, to survive and to thrive so I can use every moment to make the world a better place. And to finally, finally stop running from the past. To do everything possible to redeem it, and then let it go. I can make the choice that all of us can make. I can't ever change the past. But there is a life I can save: It is mine. The one I am living right now, this precious moment.

I am ready to go. I take a stone from the ground, a little one, rough, gray, unremarkable. I squeeze the stone. In Jewish tradition, we place small stones on graves as a sign of respect for the dead, to offer mitzvah, or blessing. The stone signifies that the dead live on, in our hearts and memories. The stone in my hand is a symbol of my enduring love for my parents. And it is an emblem of the guilt and the grief I came here to face—something immense and terrifying that all the same I can hold in my hand. It is the death of my parents. It is the death of Eric and the life that was. It is what didn't happen. And it is the birth of the life that is. Of Béla and our family. Of the patience and compassion I learned here, the ability to stop judging myself, the ability to respond instead of react. It is the truth and the peace I have come here to discover and all that I can finally put to rest and leave behind.

I leave the stone on the patch of earth where my barrack used to be, where I slept on a wooden shelf with five other girls, where I closed my eyes as "The Blue Danube" played and I danced for my life. *I miss you*, I say to my parents. *I love you. I'll always love you.*

And to the vast campus of death that consumed my parents

and so very many others, to the classroom of horror that still had something sacred to teach me about how to live—that I was victimized but I'm not a victim, that I was hurt but not broken, that the soul never dies, that meaning and purpose can come from deep in the heart of what hurts us the most—I utter my final words. *Goodbye*, I say. And *Thank you.* Thank you for life and for the ability to finally accept the life that is.

We can't ever change what's happened to us. We can't alter the past or control what's coming around the next corner. But we can choose how we live *now*. We can choose whom and how to love.

We can choose—we can always choose—to be free.

Acknowledgments

I believe that people don't come to me—they are sent to me. I offer my eternal gratitude to the many extraordinary people who have been sent to me, without whom life wouldn't be what it is, and without whom this book wouldn't exist.

Writing my first book was a dream come true. Publishing a third book is beyond what I ever thought possible. I couldn't have done it without my extraordinary literary team, the people who, word by word and page by page, helped me bring this book into being:

Doug Abrams, world-class agent and world's truest mensch—thank you and your dream team at Idea Architects (in particular, Jordan Jacks) for creating books that are instruments of healing. Your presence on the planet is an absolute gift.

Esmé Schwall, my co-writer—you didn't just find the words. You became me. Thank you for your ability to see my healing journey from so many different perspectives, and for turning my life into poetry.

I would like to thank Jordan Engle, my grandson, who didn't let me give up on my desire to write a book for young audiences, who guided and shepherded this project, and who supports my work and legacy.

The wise and talented Reka Simonsen and her dedicated team at Atheneum—thank you for bringing such powerful conviction, compassion, and vision to this project.

My extraordinary British publishers, who played such an important role in sharing my life and my work with the global English-speaking world, especially Judith Kendra, Olivia Morris, and Anna Bowen of Rider, Andrew Goodfellow and Joel Rickett of Ebury, and their entire wonderful team. Thank you for making *The Choice* an international success, encouraging me to write *The Gift*, supporting this book with such heart and enthusiasm, and gifting readers all over the world with books for a better life.

My wonderful global rights team: Caspian Dennis and Sandy Violette at Abner Stein; and Camilla Ferrier, Susie Nicklin, Jenna McDonagh, and Brittany Poulin at the Marsh Agency; and my truly extraordinary and devoted publishers around the world—thank you for bringing my work to readers of many countries and languages.

I am blessed with so many friends, colleagues, and healers who enrich and support my daily life, in particular:

Wendy Walker, an inspirational role model of how to be a true survivor and live in the present.

Bob Kaufman, Lisa Kelty, Debbie Lapidus, Sid Zisook, and so

many more inspirational colleagues—thank you for the years of insight and conversation, and for the healing you bring to those who are suffering. You revive and renew so many lives, including mine.

Katie Anderson, my right-hand woman, who keeps me on top of everything, supports me in tackling anything, and models how to be a take-charge person.

Dr. Scott McCaul and Dr. Sabina Wallach, who have never doubted my strength to endure.

All of my love and gratitude to my family:

Magda and Klara, my beloved sisters. I could not have survived without you. May you forever know how much I love you and how much you are missed.

Béla. Life mate. Soul mate. Father of my children. Loving, committed partner who risked it all to build a new life with me in America. Our rich life together was a feast. I love you.

My son, John Eger, who has taught me how not to be a victim and who has never given up the fight for people living with disabilities.

My daughters, Marianne Engle and Audrey Thompson, who have offered me unceasing moral support and loving comfort, whose edits and insights on all three books helped bring my story and perspective on healing to life on the page, and who understood, perhaps before I did, that it would be more difficult for me to relive the past than it was to survive Auschwitz. In Auschwitz, I could think only about my survival needs; to write this book, I had to feel all the feelings. I couldn't have taken the risk without your strength and love. Thank you for all the ways you've helped me grow.

My grandchildren, Lindsey, Rachel, Jordan, David, and Ashley, who are ambassadors of peace, living proof that life is beautiful, that my parents didn't die in vain. May you keep passing on the love and strength of our family.

My children's and grandchildren's beautiful spouses and life partners, the people who keep adding branches to the family tree: Rob Engle, Dale Thompson, Lourdes, Justin Richland, John Williamson, and Illynger Engle.

When our first grandchild was born, Béla said, "Three generations—that's the best revenge to Hitler." Now we are four! Thank you to the next generation—Silas, Graham, Hale, Noah, Dylan, Marcos, and Rafael. Every time I hear you call me GG Dicu, my heart goes pitter-patter.

My nephew Richard Eger—my Dickie-boy—and his wife, Byrne, and my niece Annabelle Eger Sher and her husband, Richard, thank you for being true relatives, for watching over me and my health, and for celebrating holidays together.

To Magda's daughter, Ilona, and her son, Grant, and to Klara's daughter, Jeanette, and her daughter, Charlotte, I get chills when I see my parents and sisters in you, and as I watch your unique selves bloom. Thank you for sharing the journey.

To all of you who have touched my life, had faith in me, guided me not to give up—to every person who has moved, inspired, and nourished me—I celebrate your one-of-a-kind gifts and cherish your presence in my life. Thank you for replenishing my basket and helping me take responsibility for my life and my freedom. I have never felt so blessed and grateful—or so young! Thank you.